Remembering Bear

Remembering Bear

By the Staff of The Birmingham News

News & Features Press, Indianapolis, Indiana 46220
1983

Photo and text credits:

Cover design by *Birmingham News* editorial art director Ray Brown.

Front cover photographs by *Birmingham News* photographic chief Robert Adams; back cover photograph by *News* staff photographer Bernard Troncale.

Material for **Remembering Bear** was taken from the pages of *The Birmingham News*. Some of the stories by the late *News* sports editor Benny Marshall, after being published originally in *The News*, later appeared in a book, **Winning Isn't Everything,** published by Parthenon Press. Those portions of **Remembering Bear** are reprinted with permission of Marshall's widow, Mrs. Ruth Marshall Jordan of Bessemer.

Contents

Paul Bryant hugs player who years later will replace him as head coach, Ray Perkins.

Introduction

The words of a song ask: "Where have all the heroes gone?"

When Paul Bryant died on Wednesday, Jan. 26, 1983, another American hero was taken from us.

For 25 years *The Birmingham News* helped record the story of this giant of a man who dominated not only his chosen profession but to a very large extent the life of a state.

Bear Bryant was the winningest coach in the history of collegiate football, but to dismiss him with that label is to dismiss the Queen Mary as a big boat.

Bryant was, as much as anything else, a symbol of the American dream. He was the poor boy who made good and, moreover, he made good in a bruising sport that is only for the manly.

Bryant was the 11th-born of 12 children of the Wilson Monroe Bryant family. His father was a semi-invalid, and his mother rode a peddling wagon. There were no extras at the Bryants' house in Moro Bottom, near Fordyce, Ark.

Yet, when Bryant died he was a wealthy man, and his name was known to most Americans. He was the famous friend of the famous, numbering such as Bob Hope, Arnold Palmer and Gerald Ford among his pals.

His mother wanted him to become a preacher, but he told her preaching and coaching were similar. And, of course, one reason for his success was his ability to motivate. "We almost tore the door off the dressing room when it came time to go out on that field," has been spoken so many times by reminiscing ex-Alabama players that it has become a cliche.

As the old verities seemed to more and more lose currency in a changing America, Bryant remained a pillar of the work ethic. There were no short cuts to excellence, he said, and so he put in long hours. His assistants and players knew he didn't ask them to do anything he wouldn't do — and hadn't done (he once played with a broken leg).

The image grew in the 1960s when Bryant's "itty-bitty boys" won national championships by beating much larger opponents. Their success was simply further evidence that hard work had its rewards.

And what more irrefutable evidence than the man winning his 315th game in 1981 to surpass Amos Alonzo Stagg as the winningest coach?

Bryant was living in Fordyce, where his mother ran a boarding house, when he discovered football. He was an eighth grader watching the varsity practice, and he told the coach he didn't know how to play football. The safetyman was catching punts, and the coach said it was simple, "you go down there and try to kill him." Bryant destroyed the poor safety, and the following Friday he was in the starting lineup, and a career was born.

The University of Alabama recruited him, and he played end. Bryant in later years scoffed at his playing ability, but he was a second-team All-SEC choice in 1934.

Bryant's coaching career began as an Alabama assistant, and at 32 he became head coach at Maryland. Stints at Kentucky and Texas A&M followed before he heeded "Mama's call" in 1958 and returned to Alabama as head man.

Thus began the greatest period in the athletic history of the university. Alabama football became synonymous with excellence.

They were good years for the school and for the state. *The Birmingham News* is proud to offer this collection of stories and pictures — this collection of memories, to be cherished for a lifetime by a legion of friends and admirers — of the life of Paul William (Bear) Bryant.

James E. Jacobson
Editor, *The Birmingham News*

Paul Bryant in football uniform.

Bryant: A winner's journey

"Arkansas is not my home," Paul Bryant told some friends one day. "Alabama is. Alabama is where I've bought my cemetery lot."

Indeed, the Alabama days were the peak ones for Paul William "Bear" Bryant, who died in Druid City Hospital in Tuscaloosa after suffering a massive heart attack.

It had been only a few weeks since Bryant made headlines by retiring as the University of Alabama's head football coach after the Tide beat Illinois, 21-15, in the Liberty Bowl in Memphis Dec. 29, 1982.

But it was his childhood in Arkansas that formed the bedrock of the motivation that led Bryant to become college football's winningest coach. He was the 11th of 12 children of the Wilson Monroe Bryants. His father was a semi-invalid, and things were tough in Moro Bottom near Fordyce, Ark.

As a child he accompanied his mother on her peddling wagon, selling milk, butter, eggs, turnip greens, blackeyed peas, watermelons and other produce. In the winter she heated bricks to keep the youngsters from freezing in the wagon. Sometimes, when there was a lot of rain, the wagon would actually float over Moro Creek, and for the rest of his life Bryant marveled at the mules Pete and Joe, swimming that creek while pulling the wagon.

What exactly was Moro Bottom? "Metropolitan Moro Bottom consisted of six families spread over a two-mile area," Bryant said.

Bryant was born on Sept. 11, 1913, to Ida Kilgore Bryant whom he called "my favorite person in the world," and she was the rock upon which his character was formed. "You could look at her and tell she had class, despite all she had been through," he said.

With her husband ill, Ida Bryant also was the disciplinarian of the family. When young Paul tossed a cat through a window of a church in which a revival was being held, an act that elicited a squeal from a girl in whose lap it landed, it was Mamma who dusted his britches.

Neither of Bryant's parents ever saw a football game. Years later, when he took teams to bowl games, his mother went along, but she stayed in the hotel room.

Bryant and some of his cronies walked from Moro Bottom to the Lyric Theater in Fordyce one summer day. On the front of the hall was a picture of a bear, and the offer of a dollar a minute to anyone who would wrestle the bear. "For a dollar a minute I'd do anything," Bryant said, glancing at a pretty girl who was looking at the poster. He was chopping cotton for 50 cents a day at the time and was about 13 years old.

The proprietor of the theater agreed to let Bryant and his friends in free if he would wrestle the bear.

They brought the bear onto the stage. One of his pals in later years recalled it was "a mangy, little old bear." Bryant said it looked 30 feet tall.

All Bryant knew about wrestling was that if a person got hold of the opponent and kept his body away, the foe would have difficulty breaking the hold.

When the bear reared up, Bryant charged him and immediately took him down so that he couldn't move. There they lay. The show was flopping. The promoter told Bryant to let the bear up, but time was ticking by and he was, he thought, earning money. "I just lay there," Bryant remembered.

The bear worked loose and Bryant got him again and he worked loose again and Bryant's eyes popped when he saw the muzzle was gone. He felt a burning on his ear, and when he touched it he got a handful of blood.

Bryant leaped from the stage and crashed into the front row of seats, and that left marks on his shins that stayed with him throughout his life.

When the movie was over, Bryant went to get his money. But the man who owned the bear had flown the coop. He got something more valuable, though, a lifelong nickname — Bear.

Fordyce High School Redbugs, 1930 Arkansas State Champions.
Paul Bryant is second from right on the line.

Years later, when Bryant was an assistant coach at Alabama, he encountered the man at a carnival. He stifled the urge to choke his money out of him.

Eventually his mother rented a big house in Fordyce and took in boarders. One day when Bryant was in the eighth grade, he walked by the field where the high school team was practicing football. He had never seen a football before.

Even though he had never even seen a football before, he accepted the coach's challenge to "kill" the safetyman. Bryant ran over the safetyman, and the following Friday he was a starter on the team.

His mother took his high-top shoes to a cobbler who put cleats on them. They were the only shoes he had, and he wore them to football practice, to class, to Sunday school. Bryant was proud of those shoes.

Years later, when he was head coach at Kentucky, Bryant wasn't getting anything out of his quarterback, George Blanda. One day Bryant noticed cardboard in the bottom of Blanda's shoes. He told him to go to a clothing store and buy a new outfit, head to foot, and charge it to him. Kentucky didn't lose a game.

Bryant played offensive end and defensive tackle at Fordyce High. One of Fordyce's opponents was Pine Bluff High, which featured a superb end named Don Hutson.

Bryant was enamored of the University of Alabama. He had heard about the Crimson Tide and Wallace Wade who had taken his men to three Rose Bowls. The Arkansas head coach took Bryant to Dallas to a college all-star game, but at the half Bryant slipped out and listened to Alabama beat Washington State 24-0 in the 1931 Rose Bowl.

Bryant hadn't finished high school when he arrived on the campus of the University of Alabama in 1931. He needed to study a language, so he attended Tuscaloosa High and practiced with the Alabama team. Wallace Wade left the year before Bryant came, and Frank Thomas was the head coach who molded him into a college player.

Bryant in later years belittled his playing ability, saying he was merely "the other end" opposite the great Don Hutson.

But, as a matter of fact. Bryant made second team All-Southeastern Conference in 1934, the year Hutson made All-America.

"As far as all-around play, I suspect

Paul Bryant, 1946.

he was as good as any we have had," said Red Drew, who coached Alabama's ends when Bryant played and who later became head coach. "Defense was his long suit. He liked to get at them. He was a great blocker, and when we threw the ball to him he'd catch it. Dixie Howell's main target was Don Hutson, but Bryant could do everything he needed to do."

Grantland Rice said Bryant would make All-America in 1935, but he suffered a broken leg and didn't.

In the second game of the season, against Mississippi State, the senior end left with a broken leg in the first period. He returned in the third quarter and finished the game. No one knew it was a fracture, but they knew

the next week.

Bryant made the train trip to Knoxville with his leg in a cast and on crutches. But he got the cast off, started and played against Tennessee until Alabama had the game in the bag.

"It was just one little bone," Bryant said years later.

"Well, how many bones do you need for a broken leg?" Drew countered.

As a player, Bryant was the prototype of the coach he would become. Frank Thomas recognized that and hired him as an assistant coach when his playing days ended. On June 2, 1935, Bryant was married to a campus beauty, Mary Harmon. They would have two children, Mae Martin and Paul Jr.

Bryant and Hutson opened a dry cleaning place. Alabama got new uniforms in 1938, and Bryant sent them to his place for cleaning. The jerseys shrank several sizes and couldn't be used, but Coach Hank Crisp covered for him and ordered new ones.

Bryant moved from Alabama to Vanderbilt as Red Sanders' No. 1 assistant in 1940. After the 1941 season he was invited to be interviewed for the head coaching job at Arkansas.

He was returning to the state which he had left for this game that would dominate his life. Sure enough, the job was his. He was only 28 years old.

Bryant was driving back home, and he was proud. But the day was Dec. 7, 1941, and the car radio told him the Japanese had bombed Pearl Harbor. He kissed his wife hello, kissed her goodbye, and the next day he was in Washington and soon he was in the Navy. Somebody else would have to be head coach at Arkansas.

Bryant attained the rank of lieutenant commander and went to North Africa, but he was never in any fighting. He coached at North Carolina Pre-Flight at Chapel Hill.

George Marshall, owner of the Washington Redskins, offered Bryant an assistant's job, but Bryant said he wanted to be a head coach. Marshall called Curly Byrd, president of the University of Maryland, recommended Bryant (who had been a part-time scout for the Redskins in earlier years), and Byrd hired him. At 32, Bryant was a head coach.

He was discharged from the Navy five days before Maryland's opening game. He took 17 members of the North Carolina Pre-Flight team with him, and they were the heart of the squad.

Maryland had won only one game the season before, but Bryant won six of nine, beating little Guilford 60-6 in the opener.

After Maryland beat Virginia — which had won 16 in a row — Byrd told a contractor to build Bryant the finest home in Maryland, that he had a lifetime contract.

But reality set in. Byrd fired one of Bryant's assistants without telling him and reinstated a player Bryant had kicked off the team. Bryant knew he must quit.

He picked up a bunch of telegrams off his desk and went home and cried like a baby. Finally, he went through the telegrams - and there was one offering him the head coaching job at Kentucky.

Coach Bryant with his friend, Homer Thomas, 1947.

Maryland students, angered at Byrd, went on strike. Bryant headed for Kentucky, worried lest the people in Lexington think him a rabble rouser. When he arrived he was greeted by a crowd, and he thought they were going to bar him. Then he saw a welcome sign.

At Kentucky, Bryant found "big, fine-looking boys who wallowed around and wouldn't play." But Bryant got the show on the road immediately, forging a 7-3 record his first year. A number of ex-servicemen, some older than Bryant, were on the club, and in Knoxville before the Tennessee game a waiter refused to serve Bryant coffee, saying he'd have to drink milk like the other players.

The fear of having to return to the peddle wagon still haunted Bryant, and

he got about four hours of fitful sleep a night, working constantly. Pat James, an assistant, remembers a meeting that lasted until 4 a.m.

Bryant's Kentucky teams were typically hard-nosed. "Playing for Bryant was like going to war," George Blanda said, "You may come out intact, but you'll never forget the experience."

Bob Gain, a superb tackle, was a discipline problem, but he straightened out to become a fine leader under Bryant's driving. Gain went to Korea shortly after he got out of UK, and the night before he was going into battle he wrote Bryant a letter, telling him he used to hate him. But, he said, "I love you tonight for what I used to hate you for."

Kentucky won 60, lost 23 and tied five during Bryant's eight seasons there.

Winning coach Paul Bryant with three of his Kentucky players following the 1952 Cotton Bowl.

The Wildcats — who had never been to a bowl before — played in the Great Lakes, Orange, Sugar and Cotton bowls under him.

Even Bryant could make a mistake — and laugh about it.

"This story goes back a ways," Bryant told it years later. "It was in 1948 at Kentucky. We lost three in a row then beat Marquette, and Cincinnati was next. We were 14-point underdogs.

"We got out to the stadium and dressed and went out to warm up. I noticed Cincinnati wasn't out yet, and I thought to myself, 'Now what are they trying to pull?' That Sid Gillman is tricky.

"Cincinnati still hadn't shown up when we went in. I knew it was a trick now. The players were inside, milling around. I told 'em to sit down, like you will, and I was walking back and forth, like I do, just waiting.

"I was wondering, too. Then I went in the back and for some reason looked at my watch, and it struck me like lightning what had happened. I had been thinking they were on Eastern Daylight Time; they were on Eastern. I had taken my football team out there early, one whole hour.

"No, I didn't say anything. What would you say? I just kept walking and walking and my players kept sitting. Man, I must have walked nine miles, waiting.

"Finally, it was time. Now you've

heard of football teams tearing down the door to get out of a dressing room. That's what my Kentucky team did. Did we win? Sure we did, 28-7. And after the game when I was talking with Gillman he asked me, 'What's this you're doing, coming out early like that?' I just went on; I sure wasn't going to tell him what had happened.

"In fact, I never did plan to tell anybody about it. It was, I guess, eight or 10 years later when Carney Laslie and Frank Moseley — they were assistant coaches there — were talking about it one night. They said it was the greatest job of psychology they had ever seen worked by a coach getting his team ready to play.

"Psychology my eye! I had to tell them then."

Kentucky was not big enough for Bryant and Adolph Rupp, the basketball coach. "The trouble was, we were too much alike," Bryant said. "He wanted basketball No. 1, and I wanted football No. 1."

Bryant said he got "pigheaded" and left Kentucky, and he called it "probably the most stupid thing I ever did."

Bryant had several offers while he was at Kentucky, but the only one open when he quit was from Texas A&M, a tough place to lure players to. No girls, no glamour, military uniforms and, at first glance, the look of a penitentiary.

Bryant early on encountered the dif-

ficulty of recruiting there. No one wanted to come. Finally, Bryant dispatched an assistant to the late-summer Alabama High School All-Star Game to see if anyone was unsigned. The assistant reported there was only one unsigned

Paul Bryant, coach of the Texas Aggies, 1954-57.

all-star who possibly could play — and he had only one arm.

A&M signed him anyway, and Murray Trimble made all-conference guard. His brother Wayne later played for Bryant at Alabama.

One who wanted to play for Bryant — but not A&M — was Don Meredith, who starred at SMU and for the Dallas Cowboys. "Coach, if you were anywhere in the world except A&M," Meredith said with tears in his eyes.

But Bryant won at A&M. His record in four years was 25-14-2, and his third squad won the Southwest Conference title, though it didn't go to the Cotton Bowl because A&M was on probation for recruiting violations.

Bryant didn't win right away, though. His first team went 1-9, and it was the only losing year he ever had as a head coach.

Bryant took two busloads of players to Junction, Tex., for camp that September and returned with less than half a load — 29 boys. "The quitters outnumbered the players three to one," Bryant said.

A reporter told Bryant his sports editor had heard there was dissension on the squad.

Answered the coach: "Well, you call your boss and tell him I said if there isn't any dissension now there's damn sure going to be in a hurry, and I'm going to cause it."

All six centers quit, and a sophomore guard volunteered to switch to the pivot. A manager suited up to center the ball on punts.

Texas Tech stomped the Aggies 41-9 in the opener, and the only game they won was a 6-0 affair over Georgia after an A&M assistant noticed in films that the Georgia quarterback gave away the play by the position of his feet.

One of the players who stayed was John David Crow, who later would win the Heisman Trophy and serve on Bryant's staff at Alabama.

Bryant's 1957 A&M club lost to Tennessee in the Gator Bowl, but the news long since had leaked that he was returning to Alabama. In fact, it had been formally announced before the bowl.

"You don't stay at Texas A&M as long as we did without learning to love it, the tradition, the boys, everything," Bryant said. "The reason, the only reason, I'm going back is because my school called me."

Total dedication football produced its casualties in 1958 at Tuscaloosa. A

Mr. & Mrs. Paul Bryant, 1958.

number of players quit the first three days, some of them men with the most ability. "If a man's a quitter, I want him to quit in practice, not in a game," Bryant said. "There has been enough of that."

LSU, a team armed with Billy Cannon and headed for the national championship, was Bryant's first opponent. The Tigers figured to be able to name the score, but LSU won by only 13-3 after being held scoreless in the first half.

Alabama lived by defense in that first game, and for years that would be a Tide trademark. The tally at the end of the first season was 5-4-1. That was more games than Alabama had won in the previous 36.

Bryant's second squad went 7-2-2 and earned a trip to the Liberty Bowl — thus establishing a tradition of visiting a bowl every year.

The AP and UPI national championships fell to Bama in 1961 as the Tide went 11-0 and beat Arkansas in the Sugar Bowl. The club allowed only 25

points, fewest since Frank Thomas' 1933 squad gave up 17. It was a defense that featured Lee Roy Jordan. The quarterback was Pat Trammell, the man Bryant called the greatest leader he ever coached.

Joe Namath succeeded Trammell as Bryant's quarterback, and he would become the most famous player ever to play at the Capstone. Namath threw three touchdown passes in his first game, a 35-0 lashing of Georgia, but the game would become more famous as the subject of a 1963 *Saturday Evening Post* article charging that Bryant and Georgia Athletic Director Wally Butts had conspired to "fix" it.

It was an expensive story. Both sued. Bryant earlier had sued over a *Post* article that charged him with brutal coaching methods. After the case went all the way to the Supreme Court, Butts finally was awarded $460,000 plus interest. Bryant received a $300,000 settlement from Curtis Publishing Co.

Coach Paul Bryant and quarterback Joe Namath, 1964.

Johns in the 170 class.

The 1960s ended with Alabama the Team of the Decade and Bryant the Coach of the Decade. The Tide won 90, lost 16 and tied four for the best record in the country. An NCAA poll decided Bryant had done the best coaching job.

Another national title came to Alabama in 1973, the UPI version, but it had a hollow ring because Notre Dame beat the Tide in the Sugar Bowl in a battle of unbeatens and took the AP trophy. It was the first of four Irish whippings of the Tide in matches between college football's two biggest names.

The 1978 Alabama used a famous goal line stand against Penn State in the Sugar Bowl to win the AP's national championship. The next season, rolling 12-0 and downing Arkansas 24-9 in the Sugar Bowl, the Tide took both wire service national titles.

The 1981 season saw Bryant become the winningest coach in the history of college football. His victory over Auburn was his 315th, which broke a deadlock with Amos Alonzo Stagg.

Bryant announced on Dec. 15, 1982, he would retire as Alabama's head coach. He remained as athletic director until he died. His overall coaching record was 322 victories, 85 losses and 17 ties.

Clyde Bolton

Namath guided Alabama to AP and UPI national titles in 1964, but not before Bryant booted him off the 1963 club for the final two games, a regular season match with Miami and the Sugar Bowl against Ole Miss.

"I'll guarantee you I never had a gut check over a boy like I had with Joe Namath," Bryant said. He learned his starting quarterback had been drinking and gave him the boot. Steve Sloan led the team to victories in the final games.

Sloan quarterbacked an AP national championship squad in 1965, and Ken Stabler succeeded him in 1966. That team went undefeated but lost the national crown to a Notre Dame team with an inferior record.

The 1964, '65 and '66 teams were famous for their lack of size. Men such as Jerry Duncan, John Calvert, Bruce Stephens, Paul Crane and Wayne Owen were starting linemen at under 200 pounds. There were linebackers such as Bob Childs who weighed less than 180 and defensive backs such as Dicky Thompson, John Mosley and Bobby

1969 Alabama Sports Hall of Fame inductees Johnny Mack Brown, Joe Louis, Paul Bryant, Don Hutson, Shug Jordan.

Bryant: The man

Walter Lewis gets a pat on the back from the coach,

Coach Bryant learned that he had been named Citizen of the Year by the Alabama Broadcasters Association while engaged in a round of golf, 1967.

There was something magnificent in the possession of Paul William Bryant, teacher of a game to young men.

All of us owned a piece of him, like it or not, like him or not.

In his last years, in turbulent times, self-doubt rampant, he became, more than anyone, America's folk hero.

He had been for years before that, and he sensed it, the most impelling voice in Alabama's conscience, with his work-ethic standard, poise, fairness and class.

Ah-h-h, how he loved that word: Class.

He knew how to spell it, which was unimportant. He knew what it meant, which was important.

He knew how to implant it, and he did, which was even more important.

There was also style.

There are also memories, priceless for so privileged many. One should be self-conscious imposing his on yours.

Bryant stories and experiences form a common treasury. Whoa! Make that last adjective 'uncommon'.

Legends are not common. He was, and friends can visualize him wincing under that resounding reminder to him, a legend.

Little stories illustrate the big man as well as large ones. Share one, please, from a Tuesday conversation.

Marguerite McWhorter, Mary Ruth Burgess, Mary Lindahl, Rose Poist and several other beautiful ladies are again dedicated to a 'roast' to benefit Multiple Sclerosis research. It's Febuary 24. It'll star Jerry Pate, golfer-swimmer.

Class was Bryant's magnificent possession

Paul Bryant is box-office. He established a record gate eight years ago as target of their first fun event.

Bryant and Pate are friends, have been since the minute Pate put on red and white as a freshman Tide golfer.

Everyone wanted Bryant's shoulder to his, or her, wheel. You know why. He'd make it turn. Demands on his time, his energy were unceasing. No public man I know, outside the ministry, gave of himself more unselfishly.

"Coach," a middleman requester was asking a friend whom he heard doctors plead to remember his health, just a teeny bit, "those MS folk could sure use you. They appreciate what you've done, but . . . ."

"Aw, hell," the voice was rumbling, "I read in the paper about Jerry's deal the other day. I knew you'd be calling. I've got the date circled."

We know now, sadly, Bryant can't keep that promise. But the spirit of Bryant will. It lives.

The love of Bryant lives on, too. The Rev. Dr. Ed Kimbrough, Bryant friend of 50 years, was speaking so eloquently about that, privately, Wednesday evening.

"Love is unquenchable," said this minister of life's grander goals. "It never dies."

It was there for the enrichment of many ever since.

Alf Van Hoose

Taking a moment for memories

Raiding the personal memory bank for Paul Bryant data:

My first meal with him, year not certain, was probably 1948 or 1949. He was a young head coach at Kentucky visiting Birmingham with Mary Harmon, Mae Martin and Paul Jr. for Christmas vacation with Mrs. Bryant's folks.

He dropped into the *News* sports department around noon. Sports editor Zipp Newman had a luncheon date and assigned me to take Bryant to lunch, and do a story. Raiford Ellis, one of Bryant's Alabama teammates, was called and made it a threesome at the Redmont Hotel.

Bryant wasn't a charming companion. One sensed he wasn't excited about dealing with substitutes, socially or professionally. . . .

Another Christmas-period lunch with Bryant came several years later, he having shifted from Kentucky to Texas A&M, this time at Frank Merrill's Charcoal Steak House across from *The News* Building.

"Any good high school players around here?" Bryant asked casually, early — as if he didn't know.

"Tommy Lorino of Bessemer is the best prep running back around these parts in years," he was told.

"Hm-m-m," Bryant mused.

Auburn folks told it later — and there could have been some truth in it — that Bryant visited Chico Lorino's grocery store that afternoon. Chico was Tommy's dad.

"You own this?" Bryant was reported to have asked Mr. Lorino after looking around the store and knowing that if all the merchandise were bought Chico still wouldn't have a good day.

"Yes sir," Mr. Lorino admitted.

"Well I'll tell you what you do," Auburn people said Bryant told the little owner. "You call your friends in, give 'em this stuff, send your boy to Texas A&M and hunt yourself a spot for a supermarket."

During another meal with Bryant, fresh on the job at Alabama, was an old Bryant friend and a Bama alumnus capable — financially and philosophically — of buying the Tide several franchise-type prep stars.

Whether for the third party's ears, or the newsman's — probably for both — Bryant pronounced his recruiting creed for Alabama.

There was no doubting sincerity this time. His voice was rock-edged, and clear:

"The scholarship at Alabama is for room, board, books and $15 a month. No more, no less.

"I'll do the recruiting, me and the staff. If we want help from anybody, I'll let it be known.

"I've been the other route. No more. Anybody who promises any player a dime more than what is legal will be cut off from any connection with the athletic program as long as I'm there."

Then there was a telephone conversation to Bryant from Atlanta, just minutes after a federal jury had smashed all records for libel judgments by awarding Wally Butts $3.06 million from Curtis Publishing Co.

Bryant had a suit pending against Curtis for the same *Saturday Evening Post* article charging Bryant and Butts "fixed" a Georgia-Alabama football game.

Butts had sued for $10 million. He'd been happy for $1. That would have cleared his name.

The previous libel-damage ceiling had been about $500,000 to Quentin Reynolds from columnist Westbrook

Coach Bryant's 52nd birthday, 1964.

Bryant's 65th birthday; a surprise party by Birmingham's TD club.

Pegler and his publishers.

So now the Butts jury was in and the Butts family was celebrating in the courtroom. A call was placed to Tuscaloosa for Bryant's reaction to the tremendous settlement and victory.

"Coach," the reporter said, "Wally just won."

"Good," Bryant replied. "What'd he get?"

"Three million, 60 thousand," Bryant was told.

Silence for a couple of seconds. Then that low rumble again:

"What happened to the rest of it?"

There was another breadbreaking with Bryant. Benny Marshall was there, in the Bankhead Hotel Coffee Shop, and Ruby Trigg had just served the party of three eggs, grits, fried fatback and biscuits.

In a week or so Bryant would be starting 1967 September practice, his Alabama coming off an 11-0-0 1966 season (but no national championship for his best team ever). The Tide was favored to win the '67 national crown.

The game's finest quarterback — though few recognized him, officially — had been suspended during spring training for academic and other shortcomings.

Kenny Stabler had been told to get his grades in shape during summer school, conform to team social disciplines, and ask Bryant and the squad for another chance before fall practice.

Stabler did all three things. Bryant was discussing the decision only he, as commander, would have to make.

Richie Mewbourne and Coach Paul Bryant making plans for Cerebral Palsy fund drive, 1977.

"I'm going to make a mistake," Bryant said. "I'm probably going to let him play.

"He's come to me a half-dozen times in the past, after some silliness with that little ole choirboy smile and promised me he'd straighten up.

"If I take him back, we'll have a heckuva team but it'll wreck the program for two or three years afterwards.

"If I kicked him off, as I know I should, after all those times I've forgiven him after he served his punishments, it'll probably ruin him. He's got so much ability.

"One man doesn't make a team. It takes 11. I make decisions with the team in mind first. But if I can get through to that young man . . . I don't know. I don't know."

As you might recall, prodigal Stabler was allowed back, though told he wouldn't be first string the first game.

Joe Kelley started against Florida State. FSU immediately went up, 14-0.

Stabler rushed off the bench and had a terrific night, Bama and FSU tying finally, 37-37.

Alabama went 7-1-1 into its Auburn game and Stabler won it, 7-3, with a memorable mud TD run of some 45 yards.

Stabler went on to a Hall of Fame pro career.

Alabama went in reverse—to 8-3 in 1968, 6-5 in 1969 and 6-5-1 in 1970.

Alf Van Hoose

"Don't ever give up on ability. Don't give up on a player who has it."

Coach Bryant meets with President John F. Kennedy after winning his first national championship. From left are Bryant, John Cochran of NBC, Alabama quarterback Pat Trammell, Alabama President Dr. Frank Rose, Kennedy, Mel Allen, Young Boozer, former News sports editor Benny Marshall, Tom Russell and Jeff Coleman, 1961.

Hail from the chief

Dr. Frank Rose, Alabama's president; Paul Bryant, Jeff Coleman and Pat Trammell, the great quarterback, were Alabama's official delegation to the Hall of Fame dinner in New York Dec. 6, 1961. There they would receive the MacArthur Trophy to go with all the other honors earned by a national championship football team, and the appearance of President John F. Kennedy to congratulate Alabama's student body back home was a tremendous addition to the program. A newspaperman needed to be there. It was too late for security clearance. Perhaps now I'll go to jail but for one night I was "Dr. Marshall" of the University of Alabama board of trustees, who had come in unexpectedly during the afternoon. Dr. Rose showed no inclination to make the appointment permanent, however.

It was 7:30 in New York, which is 6:30 in Alabama.

Outside, the big town swirled up and down in its nightly rush to get no-place in a hurry.

Inside, at the Waldorf-Astoria, the ballroom was crowded with people, and loud with voices, and big football names were a dime a dozen about the place.

It was getting right tense in Room 804, upstairs. There was a telephone to the left, and another to the right, and another hooked up to a microphone.

"That one," Tom Russell pointed, and Dr. Frank Rose, president of University of Alabama, sat down and took it up.

"Is Jeff Bennett there?" he asked, "Jeff? That band's going to have to quiet down some." He looked across the room to Paul Bryant, his football coach, who stood beside Pat Trammell, the quarterback, and grinned. "Paul, from the sound of it, we might not have a university when we get back."

Alabama's student body had gathered to render proper student-body homage to a national football championship. At Tuscaloosa, happy people waited.

"Now, this is the way we'll do it," Dr. Rose said, and he had his procedure outlined, nice and orderly. Presently, he was speaking from New York to the University of Alabama, in joy assembled.

Then Trammell was on, thanking them all, a goodlooking boy, poised, a fine football player, a good college senior from Alabama who'd be a doctor.

Coach Bryant was next, and Young J. Boozer, and Jeff Coleman, the alumni man. "Where's Mel Allen?" Dr. Rose asked, and no one knew. But in a moment, the sportscaster who is an Alabama alumnus had come beaming to the room. There was a sports writer from back home privileged to say, "Congratulations!" too, then Mel had a word, and by now, company had come.

The Secret Service detail, I suppose, was left at the door, for the President of the United States had walked in and everybody rose.

John Kennedy had a sheet of paper in his hand, and he listened as Allen talked, scratching another note or two.

Now Frank Rose, from the University of Alabama, could tell his students, and all his people, "It's my honor to present the President."

Easily, the former scrub from Harvard lifted the phone, and surely the cheer at Tuscaloosa must have been tremendous, splitting the sky. It isn't often that Presidents come to say "Well done" to a football team, and to a school.

Mr. Kennedy did that night, and he did it well. The words were standard, routine. They don't invent new ones, but for those of us standing by watching and listening the moment was electric.

"This is history, isn't it?" Jeff Coleman whispered. It was.

I don't know how long it lasted, how long the President spoke. Maybe two minutes, maybe three. They signed Room 804 off the air, he smiled around, was introduced, shook hands and exchanged pleasantries.

"Mr. President," the football coach of the University of Alabama said to him, "You're about to become the first President in history to get an Alabama football letter."

The President of the United States grinned back at the football coach: "Would you let me play, just a couple of minutes?"

"How did those Mississippi teams do?" he asked Trammell, and Pat told him how it was with Ole Miss and State.

"I was wondering what was that coach's name?" he asked Allen, who'd made reference to Paul Bryant's old coach in his talk to the cheering students back home. "Frank Thomas," somebody said, and the President nodded his head, "Yes, I remember."

It was 7:45 now, and the band below waited to play, "Hail to the Chief," so the chief went away, as quietly, quickly as he'd come. In a little while, he'd accept a medal, laugh at some Bob Hope jokes and make a speech himself. It was an intense one, urging this nation to quit watching and start playing, to stop walking and start running, to become vigorous, physically and mentally again.

There was a prayer at the end of the Hall of Fame evening which saw Alabama receive the MacArthur Trophy as the No. 1 team in the nation, and a minister asked: "God, help this man who leads us."

And in the stillness of the night, in a hotel room far from home and celebrations, I could say it, too, for the great young man with the weight of a world in trouble on his shoulders who took time out to come to Room 804 last night for the University of Alabama.

I was glad I got to shake his hand. Real glad.

Benny Marshall

Coach Bryant gets the game ball himself after his 315th win, 1981.

Bear at retirement announcement.

The high and the humble

In late December, 1961, Alabama's national champions had pitched camp in Biloxi, Miss., awaiting a Sugar Bowl date with Arkansas which they would win. The door to the room was open just a little, and maybe the man heard the typewriter clicking, or maybe he was just looking for company. He stopped and came in, and left a story in a notebook which could be pulled out and put on paper a month or so later when he was named "Coach of the Year" for the United States. For a man in the college football business, there is no higher accolade than this recognition which comes from coaches across the country. They voted; Bryant was a landslide winner. And I remembered the pigs on the road to Fordyce, Ark.

At the time, it wasn't a story to be written. Maybe it shouldn't have been at all, but . . .

Paul Bryant had come from a meeting with his football squad that night at Biloxi the week before the Sugar Bowl, and he'd ducked in out of the cold for a minute or two.

No press conference. Just a visit. Relaxing. Hidden from the telephone which rings on overtime.

The coach of Alabama's national champions had heard from home, and

Paul Jr., who had the flu, was better. It was cold in Tuscaloosa, too. Quiet talk. Easy. That's the way it was.

If Bryant's a man of many moods, as it's popular to say, this was his best. Essentially, like most all the great ones, Paul Bryant walks alone. The door isn't opened often. This night, it was. So we sat and we talked, about nothing very much, nothing special.

Somewhere along the way, it was suggested, "You've been a lucky man." And Paul Bryant could agree with that, though I think he lives by a rule which insists, most of the time, "You make your own luck."

Then he was remembering how it had been long ago, at home, in Arkansas, and he was a boy, one of 12 children with an invalid father.

"I was going to town, to Fordyce," he said, "We had 10 little pigs, and daddy gave them to me to sell. If I could get a dollar each, he would let me keep half of it.

"I couldn't have been more than 10 or 11, I don't suppose. We were still living in the bottoms. So I hitched up and started to town, and somewhere I got the wagon stuck.

"Nothing I tried would work. Finally, I guess I just sat there and cried. It didn't

Coach Bryant helps quarterback Kenny Stabler celebrate his birthday while in New Orleans for the Sugar Bowl, 1966.

look like I could do anything. I couldn't sell the pigs. I wouldn't get the money.

"I must have been there nearly all day. But finally somebody came by, and they got me out of the mud, and I drove on to Fordyce and sold those pigs in no time at all.

"Then I went home. No. I never told them the trouble I'd had. My daddy never knew.

"But I had to be lucky. You're right. It wouldn't have happened like it did if I hadn't been lucky. We'd have never moved to Fordyce. I wouldn't have played football. I never would have gotten to the University of Alabama. I've been lucky in my wife, my friend. I'd still be out there plowing somewhere if I hadn't been lucky."

He could smile at the thought, in a luxurious motel years away from the afternoon when the wagon wouldn't go,

and the pigs wouldn't be sold. And, all of a sudden, bleakness was made light, and despair became joy.

Things have had a way of coming out right for Paul William Bryant, who the previous Saturday night had stepped to the place of honor in Chicago to accept the acclamation of his fellowmen in the coaching world.

The country boy from Arkansas was "Coach of the Year."

It was a month after Time magazine had hauled out a knife for cutting, and used it, when somebody came by saying why don't you do a piece on Paul Bryant, Bryant as you know him. Bryant as he really is.

The suggestion was good, and I struggled with it, and finally gave up for then for the simple reason that after three years of the close association that our jobs brought, I couldn't sit down

then and define this man. After many years, it still was not an easy thing.

Like all of us, the "Coach of the Year" is compounded of many things. The bottom-land outside Fordyce was part of him, and would be forevermore. So were Hank Crisp, Paul Burnum, Frank Thomas, and Mary Harmon Bryant, the lovely lady who was his wife.

I think that the bottoms outside Fordyce gave him humbleness which was real and would not go away. I think they built a fire in him, too. Bryant blazed. Failure was abhorrent. He had to be first.

And his chief coaching talent might have been the ability to build the same kind of a fire in other men who worked for him and who played the game for him that Earl Blaik calls "closest to war."

"Why don't some of these writers ask us how he is?" Billy Neighbors demanded of me once. "We could tell them."

So there was loyalty. It always works both ways. Paul Bryant did not have a short memory.

Angered, and bewildered by the sudden outburst against Darwin Holt after the Georgia Tech game, it was Bryant who said, finally, "He's my boy. What would I do but stand up for him?" Any other course was unthinkable. That was Bryant, too.

As a source of news, some found him exasperating at times. If he chose not to unbend, then unbend he did not. On the other hand, he could charm the typewriter out of a man's hand, and did.

He was impatient with anything less than complete devotion to duty. Working time was for working. But there was no more enjoyable company after hours than he. The man scowled often during a football season. Often, thereafter, he

Coach Bryant unties a giant square knot to open a Boy Scout show, 1977.

"A carnival came through (Fordyce) and they had this little ol' scraggly bear. A man was offering anybody a dollar a minute to wrestle it. I got the bear pinned, holdin' on tight. The man kept whispering, 'Let him up. Let him up.' Hell, for a dollar a minute, I wanted to hold him 'til he died."

Pepper Rodgers gets a Bear hug, 1979.

laughed.

Sometimes, the adulation of the mob irritated him. Friends' praise pleased him, though he waited not for pats on the back.

He was the most supremely self-confident human being I had ever known, and that's a quality which a detractor might label arrogance. Mentally, he was tough, and that's the only word which fits, but he was a sentimentalist, too, though he wouldn't admit it.

Business associates knew him as a man who knows what's going on. His world didn't begin and end on a football field, though this was most of it.

Outside his game, Paul Bryant prospered. He made a pile of luck for himself, and success chased after him like he invented the word.

That Saturday night in Chicago, they put him up on the peak. Paul Bryant, of Alabama, "Coach of the Year." Here was the highest honor of them all.

When they called him up front of the rest, I wonder if Paul William Bryant remembered about the pigs. I know now that it was a story which wanted writing.

It takes a lot of things and a lot of days and a lot of people to make a "Coach of the Year."

Benny Marshall

City slicker, almost

Most exclusive party in the country is the Gridiron Club's annual party in Washington, a jesting, needling gathering of headliners from all over the country. Make that guest list and you have arrived. Bryant made it in April of 1964, and don't doubt that he was impressed. He took time off from spring football practice to go. There was a bit of poetic license taken in the composing of the column which touched on the visit. The man who told me first about losing his hat was the man who had knocked it off when he climbed from the cab, and the joke aimed at himself pleased Paul Bryant no end. Newspaper friends filled out the story.

Information was secured second-

> *"You can learn a lot on the football field that isn't taught in the home, in the church or in the classroom. I'm a pretty good example of that."*

hand, but I gather that Saturday night was a large night out in the life of Paul W. Bryant, coach of Alabama football. It came about in Washington, headquarters for a nation.

Something almost always happens to keep the great moments in perspective, lest a guy get too big for his britches. When Bryant climbed out of the taxicab at the door of that most exclusive of dinners which is Washington's Gridiron Club party, the top hat he wore in greatest formality made that tall one a mite too long. Off toppled the hat. The country boy from Arkansas who wore it stooped, reached, retrieved, and marched in, signing autographs along the way with all the aplomb of any city slicker you ever saw.

A fellow who was there ranked Bryant, top hat and all, No. 2 in autograph signing before the night was done, and didn't say who was first, former President Harry Truman, or might-have-been-president Richard Nixon, who came in the same door. I'd bet on Harry, but I'm a sportswriter Democrat, of course.

Much of the program put on by Washington newspapermen was devoted to the life and cashing-in of Bobby Baker, as you would have read elsewhere. It was, as customary, a nothing-sacred evening full of needles to puncture all manner of pomposity, but light-heartedly, sort of. They kid. Maybe they don't mean it.

Came the time when Bryant of Alabama was to be introduced. The coach of the Crimson Tide, the only sports man in attendance at this gathering of great names, stood to polite applause. But the house went tumbling down, caved in by laughter, when the introducer followed up with, "Don't call me. Let me call you. I don't have as much money as *Saturday Evening Post*."

Bryant was tracked down on Sunday after he had returned to home country and gotten all the reports on Saturday

Denny Stadium scrimmage.

"Yep," he confirmed, "that's about right about the hat. Don't know about the autographs. I don't think I've ever been around as many big men in my life, all at one time."

The president of U.S. Steel was there, and Harry and Dick, who said, "Hi, Bear," and S. I. Newhouse, whose vast newspaper holdings include Alabama's largest and best, and top guys from all over the country.

Many people don't know it, for pride and success cover up a lot of things, but the top guy who coached the Crimson Tide carried within him a world of humility which wore well, and was genuine.

"I don't know why they would ask me," Bryant said. "But I'm sure glad they did." He was, too, even if the entrance was bare-headed, at first.

There are governors of states who don't get invited to Gridiron Club dinners, who'd give an eyetooth. And here was the son of a farmer from Arkansas who couldn't have dreamed 30 years ago that time and circumstance would put him in this spotlight at an occasion resembling a Hollywood premiere.

If it's possible, I think Paul Bryant might have forgotten football for just a little while that Saturday night, if the people would let him.

He was a man not easily awed. He might have been this time, but he remembered that the game he played and the game he taught and the dedication he gave to it, made it all come to pass. And along about here you get involved once more with the dreams the boys of America dream.

Every now and then, they still come out good and true, and it's good that realization should come anew at a party given by a bunch of ink-stained wretches who write for newspapers. They amass no riches, but it is given to them to puncture balloons now and then. The calling is noble, and needful.

Benny Marshall

Coach Bryant is inducted into the Arkansas Hall of Fame along with Shorty Carpenter and J.L. (Nick) Carter, 1965.

A private matter

Show me the man who never shed an honest tear, whose heart never filled and overflowed, who never came to a moment and found the sweetness of it and the sadness of it almost too much to bear, and you'll have found one who is something less than mortal human being. Paul Bryant's eyes were wet, and suddenly his voice wouldn't obey him, the night in January, 1965, when he stood to say "Thank you" to the Arkansas people who honored him. Bryant's eyes weren't the only misty ones there. And he tried to apologize later. There was no need.

Joe Garagiola, the master of ceremonies, had been funny and funny some more. Joe is a very sharp fellow, which is why the New York Yankees paid him $75,000 to talk about them on television in the summer.

All the people who are called honored guests had been introduced, and three Arkansas sports heroes had been properly installed in the Arkansas Hall of Fame, with speeches and with applause. There was an Arkansas quarterback, and an Arkansas basketball

player and quarterback from the long-ago of Ouachita College. The night had gone on overtime, but no one stirred in the banquet hall full to overflowing.

Now was the time, and this is why most of them had come. Now before them, introduced by his old friend Ike Murry suddenly turned serious and laughing not at all, was the farm boy from Moro Bottom who became the famous football coach.

Here stood Bear Bryant, toughest guy in the world, and if you don't think he'd fight you to win at anything, ask them back in Fordyce where he played.

John Crow, in from Pine Bluff, waited for the words. So did Bill Dickey, Tim McCarver, Lon Warneke, Clyde Scott, Mel McGaha, Jim Benton, Frank Broyles, big names in games. Mary Harmon Bryant waited and brothers, cousins, all his kin; and Sam Bailey and Mildred, Jimmy Hinton and Jean, Niel Morgan and Mary, and Charley Thornton, the publicity man.

Bryant congratulated Broyles and the Arkansas football team, tried a joke for size, looked down at the piece of paper

he'd laid before him, looked out across his audience to a time which might have been a million years ago.

(Later, he'd say, "I think maybe I got to thinking about Mama and that old peddling wagon. I don't know what happened.")

"I'm thankful," he said, "I have more to be thankful for than anybody in the world." Then the words stopped. The brain commanded. The voice would not obey, and Paul Bryant's eyes were brimming.

The toughest guy in the world stood before friends and home-folks and kinfolks, and he had a speech to make, and couldn't make it because he was crying. How long did he wait? How do you know? Ten seconds, 30, 60? Who clocks the time a man's heart has taken from him?

Finally, Arkansas Hall of Famer Paul Bryant spoke again, slowly, deliberately, emphasizing every word, making them come out. "I am thankful to God," he said. "I am thankful for good health, so that I could work hard. I am thankful to my mother and father and my wonder-

Bryant during Kentucky era.

ful family. I am thankful to Dan Walton for starting me in football.

"I am thankful for the opportunity to play for a great coach like Frank Thomas. I'm thankful for my teammates. I'm thankful for my beautiful wife and my children. I'm thankful that I could work under Red Sanders, and I'm thankful for all the great players. Not only the All-American ones like John Crow. The ordinary ones who made themselves great, too. I'm thankful to all of you."

Then he sat down, the tough guy with the wet eyes, and the applause was a great wave sweeping across that room, louder, louder, unceasing, on and on.

They beat their hands together, and they wouldn't stop, and these eyes, too, were wet. This was affection and admiration. This was to Collins Kilgore, his cousin, "his greatest hour."

And I don't think it was for football games won, and honors piled up on top of honors, and success complete. I think it was because he came from Moro Bottom, and now for a little while he was back home again, and his heart had opened up for all of them to see. It was a private matter between Paul Bryant and the place of his birth, and it was tribute, deeply sincere, one to the other.

Arkansas applauded. The toughest guy in the world had been found out. He wasn't tough at all.

Benny Marshall

"For a little school like Fordyce (Ark.), we had terrific football teams my three years there. I played offensive end and defensive tackle, just an ordinary player, but I was in hog's heaven. I could run pretty fast and I loved to play. I loved to practice."

At the Liberty Bowl, 1982.

A genuine southern hero

Something bigger than the both of us has been going on since Coach Bryant died, and it took, of all things, a Yankee sports writer to help me get a handle on what it's about.

To be honest, I wasn't upset at first to hear that Coach Bryant had died. He had not looked well for some years, so it certainly was no great surprise. And, too, he had been given the gift of a long and full life; it was sad that he was not going to have years of pleasant retirement, but he went quickly and left his family well provided for, and there is much to be said for both.

As for being sorry, I was a lot more sorry for those men blown up in the paper mill at Pine Hill. No warning, just gone, and Lord knows what their families will do. That's tough, and that's somebody to feel sorry for.

But—and this was a strange thing—after a day or so, I started getting a tight feeling in my chest and a lump in my throat when I thought about Coach Bryant being dead. I would read the stories in the paper, and my eyes would mist up—and my eyes do not mist easily.

Something was going on here, and part of it was the reaction of other people.

There was all that national reaction, for one thing, more than I expected. The networks spent minutes on Coach Bryant, when they kiss off a war in a few seconds. *USA Today*, that new national

newspaper, ran a color picture. On the day of the funeral the Associated Press Sports Wire had about as much on Coach Bryant as it did on the Super Bowl. All the hot-shot sports columnists seemed to have something to say.

That is major national attention for a football coach—for anybody.

And then there were the reactions of his friends and players, the remembrance of his kindnesses, small and large, which set him apart as a special sort of man.

More moving than either, though, has been the reaction of ordinary people—the people who stood along the streets in Tuscaloosa as the funeral procession went by, the people who have kept going to the grave site for days after the funeral, just to look, to be there, the people at work and on the street who seemed a little sad and you didn't have to ask them what they were sad about.

These people—us, that is—had lost more than a football coach, even if he was the winningest of all, and more than a good man, for there are, happily, many good men whose passing is not so grieved.

What then had we lost?

Enter Phil Pepe of the *New York Daily News*, one of the hot-shot sports columnists. He wrote that he had never understood Coach Bryant and the way people felt about him until he met him at a Sugar Bowl game, felt his presence and knew it all had "something to do

with the South and heroes."

Which is it, exactly. Coach Bryant was and is, as President Reagan said, "A hero who always seemed larger than life," but he was more than that too. He was a Southern hero, an Alabama hero, a real one, and who else is or has been?

"(His) chief characteristics were his rapid grasp of the possibilities of a... situation, his capacity for guessing what was in the minds of his opponents and his understanding of the weaknesses. Few have excelled him in the power of arousing devotion... His high character, his moral courage, his noble nature... made him a notable figure."

Sound like a description of Coach Bryant? What it is, in fact, is part of the *Encyclopedia Britannica* entry for Robert E. Lee, perhaps the chief historical Southern hero, whose heroism was grounded not so much in his battlefield victories as in his calm acceptance of defeat. Lee, who spent more time as a college administrator (at West Point and Washington College) than as a general, and who "spent his last years teaching, by example and precept, the youth of Virginia to be good Americans."

It is a temptation to draw parallels between Bryant and Lee, both generals on the field and both leaders by example of it. Lee too, was a master at matching personnel to positions (who can imagine a better flanker than Stuart, a better sweeping halfback than Jackson, a better power fullback than Longstreet?), a superb tactician, and a winner, too—until the other side's bench strength won the fourth quarter in the trenches, literally, of Petersburg.

For those who criticize Bryant for not taking a larger part in politics generally and integration specifically, there is the example of Lee, who studiously avoided the controversies following the Civil War as unproductive, concentrating instead on encouraging individuals to do their best, whatever their situation, and urging greater reliance on education as the key to the South's future.

The parallels break down after a while—the Arkansas farm boy vs. the well-born Virginian, the gregarious coach vs. the reserved general—but what remain alike are the important qualities: the leadership, the presence, the call to greatness. And the heroism.

And the passing of a hero, a legitimate hero, warrants lumps in throats and misting of eyes, and a geniune sorrow among us.

Bill Crowe

Bryant: The coach

Coach at the chalkboard, 1973.

Relaxing during a visit to Birmingham's Rickwood Field

If you love to play

The coach of Alabama started putting his facts together a long while ago. Here's how he felt when he marched on a practice field the first day of a football season.

"It's all based on one thing," Bryant had his game figured. "And that is if you love to play. If you don't, you shouldn't be out there on a practice field.

"There's no sin in not liking to play. The boy makes a mistake who is there and not wanting it.

"So here the boy is — and I'm not just talking about a boy at Alabama. I mean a boy at Auburn, at Georgia Tech — anywhere. Assuming that he loves it, here is his opportunity to be all the time doing something he wants to do, something everybody doesn't like to do. And something, for sure, that everybody can't do.

"He has made himself a part of a big thing. He has associated himself with the best group of kids in the world, and it doesn't matter where he is. If the system is right, he's with the best group he'll ever be with, his teammates.

"He has been accepted by an institution and its alumni. He has been given an alma mater, something to tie to. In football at our level he's going to have the opportunity to go a lot of places, first-class, and perform before thousands of people, or even millions, and his family and the others he loves.

"He's getting his foot in the door for the future, gaining recognition, and he's learning some mighty important lessons about living.

"Sure there are times when he'll hate to put on that smelly uniform. That's football. There'll be times when he gets mad at his best friend, but they forget it. There'll be times when he's cussing his coach under his breath.

"He's going to have to do a lot of hard work, learning, but he's going to be having fun eating and sleeping and just being with the boys he thinks so much of. They respect each other.

"And it all comes down to those Saturdays. The band's playing and the cold shivers are running up your back, and you're a big man playing for a lot of people.

"That's when a boy KNOWS just how much it is meaning to him.

"And if he loves the game and if he gives it everything he has in him, right then he's one of the luckiest young men anywhere in the world."

• • •

Several years of observation of Paul Bryant on duty convinced me that the sight of this man, actively displeased with the work of the young ones he coached, was a sight every other man should have seen at least once before he bought his last football ticket.

Like the Taj Mahal by moonlight, perhaps; or the tower than leans in Pisa, or Churchill Downs on Derby Day in the last electric instant before the horses thunder from the starting gate.

With Coach Bryant, it came on sort of slowly.

The tall man stood atop the tower between two practice fields, a megaphone in his hands, watching everything at once. It was possible, as Lee Roy Jordan told me once, that he had eyes in the back of his head. He missed nothing.

There was a shout of encouragement for this block over here, for the pass caught over there.

Then, silence.

Where was the man with the megaphone? The megaphone was still up there. The man climbed down.

Apprehension was noted. It grew with every step he took descending the ladder. Work continued but assistant coaches appeared to be a little edgy now as they instructed.

Game preparations, 1967.

Some players attempted the impossible. How can you move forward when doom is approaching from behind? The earth doesn't tremble but you get the idea.

The coach strode out amongst them and errant ones wished they hadn't been so errant.

Coach Bryant had a voice to fit the occasion. It may have come very, very low, and sadly, as if the speaker finally had given up all hope that these unworthy students ever would master their lessons.

There was a stern voice, like the one daddy used to use; and a cajoling voice, "Won't you ever . . . ?" and a "Boy, we're going to the woodshed" voice.

Later, those who played for Bryant and are now men, remembered all notes of the scale fondly when they gathered and talked about the days that were. But at the time the response was instantaneous. They all went harder, coaches and players, and you never saw student managers run so swiftly from place to place when someone shouted "Manager!"

Mostly, this was the voice of a leader commanding complete respect, and the troops ever so much wanted it to come rumbling down from on high bringing a message of approval earned.

They learned early that devotion to the job was demanded, that lack of excellence can be excused, but lack of trying never.

Benny Marshall

Bryant with offensive coordinator Mal Moore, 1979.

Bryant shouts orders; Gene Stallings directs traffic on sideline, 1963.

Coach Bryant at practice, 1982.

Saturday morning

I asked him, "What will you do all day, the day of the game?" And Paul Bryant answered, "Why don't you come and see?" It was a November Saturday, season of 1964, Louisiana State to be played and opportunity without precedent. Who wouldn't "go and see?" Low key is the way Alabama's coach kept it; no rah-rah, no exhorting of young men to do-or-die for alma mater, but from

dawn until kickoff, standing by, you felt the urgency building in them, and when finally the time came to write of the game itself, the product of all the preparation — and the waiting — Alabama had won again. The system was calm, without hysteria, and very good.

The eighth Saturday in the 20th head-coaching year in the football life of Paul William Bryant began, like the first,

very early in the morning. Bryant couldn't sleep. It was 4:30, and the skies still had stars in them, when the big man eased out of bed, went to the window, pushed the curtain back, and looked to see what Nov. 7, 1964, had brought to Birmingham.

He went back to bed, and still he couldn't sleep, and at 6:30 he was up for good, walking softly around the room so that his wife might sleep, but she was awake, too, and they waited together as the day of the Louisiana State game at Legion Field was born.

Nothing desperate about it, Alabama's coach insisted. "Just a strange bed," he said, "I sleep lots better at home."

Howard Schnellenberger was out early, too, and Bryant met him as he went for first coffee, and they talked a little while about offense. Then Ken Donahue was by, and they talked about defense, and there was a morning paper to be read.

The day was slow getting on its feet, and Mary Harmon Bryant didn't want to wait with it. "She's gone to see the grandbabies," her husband reported at 8, and then he settled down with the wide-paged pad and pen, and this was business. This was his job. It didn't want disturbing.

"Just jotting down a few things," he said a half-hour later, "some things I didn't want to forget. Two or three plays, like that, and I had to finish up this list. Personnel. Who goes in when and where.

"Let's go for a walk," and there wasn't much to be said, so no one said anything until the two small boys spotted the tall figure in the black trousers, and checked gray sport coat, the tie with the red stripes, ambling aimlessly.

"Good morning, gentlemen," Bryant said, and extended a hand for shaking, then signed autographs and continued on his way.

"No," he answered a question. "It's not the same as it was 20 years ago. I get up for a game, sure, and I'm that way, right now, but there was a time when I'd be sick at my stomach every morning. I was sick this morning, as a matter of fact, but it's not the same."

And it couldn't be the same, actually. The Bryant of 20 years ago had things to prove. The Bryant who couldn't sleep Saturday morning, who got up early and walked, had proved them all.

The boys in the red jackets were coming from their rooms at the motel as the clock headed on toward 10, Saturday of the game. Jim Goostree, the trainer, stood between the tables. "I'll ask Mike Hopper to return thanks," he said, and Hopper and his buddies and his coach stood, heads bowed, for the prayer.

Then they were demolishing steaks, for this was the last they'd eat until dinner after LSU, and that would be back home. Bryant ate, too, with as much relish as his young friends, and when he stood, chairs scraped as the Crimson Tide came to attention.

"There are several reminders," he said, "and they aren't offered in any particular order." His voice was low, a teacher reviewing lessons, matter-of-factly, reasonably. It came out, "If they do this . . . if we do that . . . kickoffs, punt returns, defenses, offenses," and his audience gave attention undivided.

"I think you know what to do," he said, half an hour later. "I think you are capable of doing it. Remember, do your job for just six seconds, every play, and make something happen. Don't wait for it to happen. Make it happen. Do that, and we're going to win.

"If we get a bad break," he shrugged, "so what? Then we'll get a good one. If we get behind, if we get way behind, that doesn't change it. Just give six seconds,

Bryant with assistant coach K.J. Lazenby.

Bryant makes point with Assistant Head Coach Sam Bailey.

every play.

"Now, I want to go for a walk with the quarterbacks."

Joe Namath, Steve Sloan, Wayne Trimble and Buddy French left with their coach, young men charged with the utmost in responsibility. Another half hour and they were back, and Schnellenberger, Donahue, Ken Meyer, Gene Stallings and Carney Laslie gathered with the boss for their last meeting on LSU.

"This is how the personnel will be," Bryant told them, and went down his list, even unto the fourth position, and when he'd done, he asked, "Am I wrong, somewhere?" They talked some more, and then there was a change suggested, mulled over, and then another, and the meeting broke up laughing.

"Charlie (McClendon) and Pat (James) will never believe I've got the guts to do that," he said, and the signal for dismissal was, "I've got to get some stomach medicine, men. Suppose I am losing my guts?" No one supposed so.

From the bathroom issued the sound of an uncertain baritone raised in song. "Love lifted me, dah-de-dah-de-dah," Paul Bryant sang, and Billy Neighbors would know that meant trouble for someone.

At 11:30, Ben Benjamin and Jack Baldwin of the Orange Bowl came calling for some reason or other. They left at 11:50 and Bryant clapped his hat on his head, pulled his raincoat on and went after them toward the buses

waiting, loaded with football players.

"It's a dog-goned shame," he said, "I mean the weather. The biggest crowd we ever had, and get a day like this.

"Wait," to a passenger climbing on the bus with him. "You sit over there, I'm a little superstitious."

Now, Handy Ellis' motorcycle was screaming out ahead and Joe Smelley's highway patrol people were swinging into line, leading the way through the traffic thickening as the rain kept coming and the highway glistened.

Bryant sat, silently, front seat on the right. He clapped his hands together once, muttered a complaint to himself about a traffic snarl. The players' voices were low, muted. Someone laughed nervously.

The coach looked at Tank Mitchell, small guard. "Don't let one of those big boys fall on you, Tank," he said, and there were several laughs.

Then silence again, in the bus. A man outside, carrying a small boy on his shoulders, spotted the entourage and knew who was there. "Yay, yay, Bama," he yelled, and now "Roll Tide . . . Go get 'em, men" as the bus neared the stadium and the thousands gathering there.

They swung into the parking lot, past all the upraised, happy, curious faces. Somebody screamed. "Tiger meat!" No one responded.

Then they were filing off, one by one, and the last man off the bus was Bryant. Through the dressing room, out onto

Watching practice, 1966.

the field for a walk around. "Enough rain already to make the ball slick," Bryant grunted to himself, and walked along. The crowd saw him and saluted. "Hey, Bear." "Get'em, Bear." Slowly, around the field, and the sun had come out to salute the Crimson Tide.

"In the dressing room? We'll just sit and be quiet. Nothing more to say now. If we haven't done it now, it's too late." Bryant answered another question. "They're mighty big. I worry about them just blasting us out of there. Those boys (pointing to the young ones filing off the

field to go in and put on the suits and the red shirts) look like a high school team beside LSU."

He looked after them fondly, turned and studied the vast stadium filling fast with the greatest throng ever gathered to see a football game in Alabama, then turned and walked after them.

It was 1 o'clock on the eighth Saturday in the 20th head-coaching year in the football life of Paul Bryant.

Bryant went to it quietly, matter-of-factly, a veteran at work, and such tensions as now might clutch him were hid-

den inside, deep, not to be seen or told.

Poker-faced Paul Bryant went toward another autumn date with destiny, another Saturday grown tremendous.

"Good luck," a man said. "Go get them."

"Thank you," Paul Bryant said, "We'll try."

And in a little while it was 2 o'clock, and Legion Field exploded.

Benny Marshall

Alabama vs Duke, 1972.

A reunion of the "Junction boys," 1979.

Bear's worst season; 1-9 with the 'Junction Boys'

If Paul Bryant had won all his games at the rate at which he won in 1954, he would have required 315 years to beat A.A. Stagg's record.

No other college football coach is identified with winning as strongly as Bryant is. He has had only one losing season in his 37 as a head coach. But it was a doozy.

Bryant's first team at Texas A&M, the 1954 club, won only one game while losing nine.

Yet, it is one of his most famous squads: the Junction Boys.

Bryant took the team to a camp at Junction, Texas, for preseason practice. The players and coaches stayed in old quonset huts that housed the summer training program for the A&M physics and geology majors. And the work was as tough as the setting.

Recalled Gene Stallings, who played on that team and coached with Bryant at Alabama: "When we reported for fall practice, Coach Bryant told us to get a blanket, pillow and several changes of clothes because we were going on a trip. None of the players had any idea where we were going. We wound up at the Junction camp. We were out on the field each practice day before the sun came up. Then we would go have breakfast. We would have practice in the afternoon and a meeting at night. Real soon some of the players began to quit."

As a matter of fact, two busloads went

to Junction, and less than half a load returned.

Reflecting on the exodus years later, former A&M Sports Information Director Jones Ramsey said, "I was the only sports publicist in America who could list his entire roster on an 8½-by-11 sheet horizontally."

All six centers quit, and Bryant issued a uniform to a 150-pound manager who had played the position in high school.

Lloyd Hale, a sophomore guard, became the first-string center. He symbolized the team. Two years later, he made All-Southwest Conference. Two years after Junction, A&M won the conference title.

Dennis Goehring, a little guard, exemplified the grit of those who stayed. Smokey Harper, the trainer, advised

Goehring to quit because he was afraid he would be injured. Goehring looked him in the eye and said, "I'll be here when you and Bryant are both gone." And he was right; he's the president of a bank in College Station.

Texas Tech demolished Bryant's thin Aggies 41-6 in the opener, then Oklahoma State edged them 14-6. The only win was to come the next week against Georgia, a team from the conference Bryant would terrorize in later years.

Assistant Elmer Smith pored over films of Georgia games for hours. Finally, he snapped his fingers and said, "Hey, I've got something."

By watching the Georgia quarterback's feet, he could predict the plays. If his feet were parallel to the line, he was going to hand off. If one was behind the

other a pass was coming — and it would even go in the direction of whichever foot was to the rear.

Texas A&M held the Bulldogs scoreless that day. Don Kachtick intercepted a Georgia pass in the second period, and Elwood Kettler, a halfback Bryant had converted into a quarterback, threw a 16-yard pass to Stallings for the only TD of the game.

Houston, TCU, Baylor, Arkansas, SMU, Rice and Texas went on to beat A&M — by an average margin of less than seven points — but the groundwork had been laid. In three more years at College Station, Bryant fielded teams that went 24-5-2, and he left a legacy that survives to this day. It says you've got to be tough to be an Aggie.

Clyde Bolton

Bryant celebrated the 1966 Orange Bowl victory over Nebraska with Steve Sloan (left) and Ray Perkins.

A day for believers

Two faraway bowl games and powerhouse Nebraska stood between Bear Bryant's sure-enough little ole boys and a third national championship in five years. But this day the Domino Theory worked to perfection.

The things that took place on Jan. 1, 1966 in college football would have been far too improbable ever to have sold to the movies, even back in the days when all of them ended with hero and heroine in a happy clinch because everything had worked out just right, the mortgage on the ranch had been paid off, the poor boy had become president of the firm or some such.

On the night of Jan. 1, 1966 in the Orange Bowl, Alabama won its third national football championship in five years.

On the morning of Jan. 1, 1966, Alabama ranked no better than No. 3 because during the regular run of 1965

Alabama had lost to Georgia in the last minute and had been tied by Tennessee. Michigan State was No. 1 and Arkansas was No. 2, but the final vote in The Associated Press rankings — granddaddy of them all — waited until the conclusion of the bowl games because of the involvement of these three, the Spartans, the Razorbacks, the Crimson Tide.

Michigan State would finish up against UCLA in the Rose Bowl, and Michigan State was favored.

Arkansas had Louisiana State in the Cotton Bowl. Arkansas was supposed to win.

Alabama had made it to the Orange Bowl with a strong stretch run, there to meet a Nebraska team which outweighed Tidesmen 35 pounds to the man.

Paul Bryant, the coach, talked hopefully in private to his players about what could happen. They still had a shot

at the big prize, he insisted, and they believed, because Bryant inspires this kind of confidence in young men. But even Bryant must have known that the odds against this Alabama team winding up with a second straight national championship were only slightly less than astronomical.

First, Arkansas, champion of the Southwest Conference, must lose to a Louisiana State team which had been thrashed 31-7 by Alabama back in November.

Then, one of Duffy Daugherty's mightiest Michigan State teams from the Big Ten must fall to Tommy Prothro's Uclans, and certainly the Coast team didn't belong on the same field, even if more than 100,000 were coming to see them play.

And, if Arkansas should lose in the early afternoon and Michigan State should lose in the later afternoon,

At the 1966 Orange Bowl with assistant coach Howard Schnellenberger.

Alabama had to win in the balmy Miami night from a powerhouse Nebraska which many thought had the strength to pitch the Tide out into Biscayne Bay.

"We have one chance of winning this football game," a grim Bryant told writers close to him like *The Birmingham News'* Alf Van Hoose and Tuscaloosa's Charley Land two days before kickoff.

"Our only chance is to keep the football. I've told Steve (Sloan, the quarterback) to come out throwing and to keep on throwing, and (this in violation of every Bryant tenet) I don't care if we're backed up to the one-yard line. We're going to throw the ball anywhere and I mean it. They could run us out of the stadium if we don't keep the ball."

This, then, was the plan to which Alabama was committed as the sun burst out over Miami on Saturday, Jan. 1. The players slept late, before the night game, to which the Orange Bowl had committed itself the year before when Texas won from Alabama and the television ratings spiraled up, and so did the price of future contracts. In the early afternoon, they could see for themselves the beginning of the fairytale ending now developing.

First chapter at Dallas in the Cotton Bowl. Charlie McClendon, who had played for Bryant at Kentucky and coached for him, and his Louisiana State Tigers were ready. They clamped Arkansas' Razorbacks in the kind of defensive vise which characterizes McClendon teams. They won 10-7.

The second chapter was kicking off at Pasadena in the Rose Bowl, famous old steel and concrete structure, king of them all, a mammoth place but dwarfed by the mountains. They fought it out, the home boys from UCLA and the champs of the Big Ten, and this was UCLA's prize.

The crowd was filing into the Orange Bowl when the final returns came in from out West, 14-12, for UCLA, and here you are, Alabama; or, maybe Nebraska, which was No. 4 on the national list.

Sloan, the deeply devout young man from Cleveland, Tenn., who had been converted during the season into a backup passer after two years as a quarterback who'd roll out mostly, to run or to throw, tipped Alabama's hand right away. The first time the Tide got the football, on its 39, in the first quarter, Steve put the Bryant Plan into operation. He passed.

The first pitch was a seven-yarder to tackle Jerry Duncan on the Alabama tackle-eligible maneuver whose success finally would have college rulesmakers shooting at it. It took eight plays, Sloan passing, Les Kelley and Steve Bowman running, to send the Tide into a 7-0 lead. The touchdown was a 21-yard

After the Alabama-Auburn game, 1966.

pass to Ray Perkins, and David Ray kicked the point.

Late in the first quarter, Ray missed a 19-yard field goal attempt, and Nebraska struck back early in the second to tie the score. The touchdown was a 34-yard pass to Tony Jeter. Larry Wachholtz kicked. Alabama's defense was about to be penetrated for more points than a Bryant-coached team ever had allowed. No one on the Alabama side would complain about this afterward, however. Not in the least.

Alabama struck back, going 70 yards on nine plays, after a roughing-the-kicker penalty provided new life. The big gainer was a 39-yard pass from Sloan to Perkins, and the catch was a diving spectacular. This put the ball on the 12. Bowman took care of eight and Kelley stormed in and Ray made it 14-7.

The next time Alabama got the football was back on its seven. What to do from there with a seven-point lead and halftime getting close? Play it safe? Not this night. Sloan passed, right off, 27 yards to Perkins, and the express was rolling again. Dennis Homan caught a pass, Wayne Cook another, and there was an interference call on the Nebraska 11 followed by another Sloan pass to Perkins for a touchdown. Ray made it 21-7 with 1:42 remaining before intermission.

Alabama insisted on keeping the football. Vernon Newbill recovered the onsides kickoff which followed, and Sloan fired 36 yards to Perkins forthwith. On fourth down, with time fleeting, Ray kicked a 19-yard field goal. When the teams went to rest Alabama led 24-7 and would not be in real danger again.

Nebraska pulled close in the third quarter with a 49-yard Bob Churchich to Ben Gregory pass, with Gregory in the clear and all alone for the last 25 yards. A pass for a two-pointer failed, and Alabama, which had opened up Nebraska defenses with its wide-open first-half passing, capitalized now on the ground. The Tide swept 69 yards, every inch of it on the ground with the longest gain a nine-yard run by Kelley. Frank Canterbury set up the score with a seven-yarder to the one. Bowman scored, and just to demonstrate, possibly, that the air had not been forsaken, Sloan passed to Perkins for a two-point conversion.

They went into the fourth quarter with Alabama on top 32-13. Nebraska made a touchdown, driving 55 yards with Churchich sneaking the last one, and Wachholtz kicked point.

Alabama made a touchdown right back, going 55, also, with Bowman taking the last two and Ray converting. Bryant was clearing the bench now, letting everyone have fun, and Nebraska wouldn't play dead. The Cornhuskers revved up for a final touchdown on a Jeter catch of a 14-yard Churchich pass, followed by a two-point conversion.

All of this added up to 39-28 for Bryant's lightweights. Sloan set a record with 20 pass completions in 29 attempts. "The most accurate passer" Bryant ever coached gained 296 yards with them, and Perkins' 10 catches were an Orange Bowl record, too. Kelley

Bryant saluted Shug Jordan after Auburn beat Alabama, 1969.

gained 116 of Alabama's 222 yards running behind the blocks of Cecil Dowdey, Paul Crane and John Calvert.

"I've never been in a game like this before," Alabama's coach was heard saying in the wildly happy dressing room.

No one there had seen one like it, either; nor had The Associated Press voters among the millions watching on television across the nation.

In another week, they voted, and no one really had doubted the outcome of the election.

Alabama was No. 1 again because everything which had to happen did happen. If Hollywood had had it in the old days, there would have been the hero and the heroine and you know the rest. But not even Hollywood would have taken that day and that story and tried to make it sound real. It just didn't add up, but shortly after this the first of the signs appeared which would adorn the automobiles of Bryant-admirers.

They read, "I believe."

Benny Marshall

The slogan lettered in red and framed on Bryant's office wall at Alabama read: "Winning isn't everything, but it sure beats anything that comes in second."

Pat Dye and a tear for the Bear

There it was, by golly, a tear, just beginning to moisten the corner of Pat Dye's right eye. The Auburn coach — hard, demanding, downright uncompromising — was about to allow a tiny drop from the soft side of his heart find its way through the tough iron of his character.

The War Eagles had this afternoon won now. They were camped over the football, 13 seconds left before history would turn its tide, and Dye's thoughts perhaps for the briefest of moments, now have reached across Legion Field toward his battle-scarred counterpart along the opposite sideline.

Dye's Tigers were about to cash in a nine-year old debt; they would beat Alabama, 23-22, using heart more than yardage, for their first triumph since 1972 in this storied Dixie rivalry. The elation which shook this stadium and swelled around the Auburn bench came mixed, at least for Dye, with the ironic sadness of knowing that his feat had come at the expense of an old and admired friend.

For the defeated Tide, the War Eagle's celebration meant another Saturday of disappointment, lost pride and soul searching. And Dye could feel the pain which surely stirred inside the man who had turned him toward this kind of life.

So the Auburn leader — who, at 43 and in only his second season on the Plain, already has accomplished much of what he had been hired for — turned his head downward for just a second, reflecting perhaps on what all this meant to him, his players and to their rivals.

When he looked up, preparing for the ride and the cheers as he went to greet the loser, the trace of the tear was gone, and he was ready to accept what they all had won.

Afterward, though, Dye spoke of the moment and of his deep feeling for Alabama Coach Paul Bryant, a man he worked under for nine years. "This is the truth, so help me God," Dye said, "I'd rather beat anybody in the world but Coach Bryant. He's done so much for me, there's no way I could repay him.

"Coach Bryant is still the greatest coach in the business. He always has been and always will be."

Neal Sims

"Find your own picture, your own self in anything that goes bad. It's awfully easy to mouth off at your staff or chew out players, but if it's bad, and you're the head coach, you're responsible. If we have an intercepted pass, I threw it. I'm the head coach. If we get a punt blocked, I caused it. A bad practice, a bad game, it's up to the head coach to assume his responsibility."

Bryant and Auburn Coach Pat Dye on a hunting trip, 1982.

Coach Bryant with quarterback Ken Coley, 1981.

Bear's power turned boys into winners

A darkening gray shroud of sky hung over the old man, and every so often a spatter of winter rain peppered the black and white checked hat.

The game plan, permanently curled by worrying hands, hung at his side.

Legion Field's scoreboard showed 23-22 Auburn and the clock was clicking off the final seconds; Auburn's long sufferers flooded the south end zone and swarmed over the goal post; Alabama's defense called a time-out.

Amid the chaos, the old man began his walk across the field. An official stopped him and motioned to the :05 still on the clock, but the old man simply shook his head.

Even in defeat, Paul William Bryant was going to do it his way, on his time.

The final curtain was coming down, and perhaps his final moments on that stage were an unfitting end.

He strode away slowly, painfully, amid tumultuous cheers for someone else.

In a larger sense, long after the joy of

With Terry Davis, 1971.

Auburn's 1982 victory was faded, Bryant will be cheered, revered, cherished for what his career has meant to his sport, his pupils, his state.

For a quarter century, the awesome force of Paul Bryant has turned hard scrabble farm boys into men of civic and financial success; shown the nation a bright spot in this state's sometimes spotted fabric, and given Alabamians a source of wealth when so many other areas were poor.

He did it with basics. Hard work. Dedication. A Puritan ethic. A vanity, pride, fear of failure and a past not worth going back to that kept him always looking ahead, looking for recognition, looking for something better than he had yesterday.

They were not selfish things hoarded by Bryant, though he reaped acclaim and financial success as a result. They were things that came to his people and his state.

Do not make him a saint. He could be rough; hard drinking, hard playing, tough talking and sometimes downright mean.

Even Bryant himself did not comprehend it all for so many years.

Take this passage from his book. *Bear: I'll tell you how I feel. I feel (football is) more important than ever. What else have we got to tie to? Where else can we walk out there even, same everything, even, and compete?*

Let me ask you this. Have you taught your children to work? To sacrifice?

Have you taught them self-discipline? Hell, no. They don't get it in the home, they don't get it in the schoolhouse, they don't even get it in the church the way they used to . . .

Maybe the football field's the only place left. We may have already lost it everywhere else.

But why football? Why does it have to carry such a burden? That's hard for me to say because football is my life. No in between, no compromise. It's my life.

Football is different things to different people. For everybody I know it's something to tie to. Everybody can't tie to an English class. Everybody can tie to a football team. And the results are right there to see, and a lifetime of work comes down to that.

Every football game you see represents a whole lot of preparation, all the way back to the parents, when a player was a boy, on into high school and beyond, and a lot of people have had something to do with it. The equipment man, the man who mows the grass, the fans, everybody.

It touches so many people. I don't know why — whether it's because it's a contact sport or what — but it gets hold of people. Students and alumni go wild. Everybody talks about it. Presidents call to congratulate winners in the dressing room. Newspapers devote more space to it than anything.

In Alabama, you better be for football or you might as well leave. I have been in Europe, thinking I was the only American left, and had people stop me and say, 'How's Alabama gonna do this year, Bear?'

The beautiful thing about it, for me, is this. (Earlier in the 1970s) when I accepted that offer from the Dolphins and tried to resign Dr. (David) Mathews (then University of Alabama president) wouldn't have any part of it.

He said, "Paul, I'm a young guy, and I've got all these young administrators. You're the last guy I've got to hang my hat on." You know, the old man. The significance of it didn't hit me then, when it did I realized a few things.

Such depth of thought, such concerns, were not instantly dredged from Moro Bottom. Paul Bryant was once uncouthly described as "raw meat" when he arrived at Alabama from an Arkansas farm.

"I first knew Bear when he stumbled into the seventh grade at Fordyce High. And I mean stumbled," recalled Ike Murray, a six-year classmate-teammate of Bryant. "He was the countriest, awkwardest son-of-a-gun I ever knew. I was a city boy. Bear was rural, 110 percent.

"If I'd been writing the class prophecy for our senior class at Fordyce I'd written about Bear: 'He'll be lucky if he stays out of the penitentiary.'

"One thing for sure. I'd never thought he could teach anybody, anywhere."

So unhewn that close friends did not recognize his depth, Bryant nevertheless gained momentum. And he carved a path the best way he knew how: with football.

The wins and losses are all there for those who care to count them up.

While they speak of the depth of accomplishment, they do not reveal why or how it happened.

Watching practice from the tower steps, 1981.

The coach observed practice from a golf cart, 1981.

"Football has never been just a game to me," he said. "Never. I knew it from the time it got me out of Moro Bottom, Ark. — and that's one of the things that motivated me, that fear of going back to plowing and driving those mules and chopping cotton for 50 cents a day.

"If you ask me what motivates a team, makes them suck up their guts when the going is tough, I'll tell you I don't have the answers, but I know for myself I've been motivated all my life.

"I still get up at 5 o'clock. I'd like to sleep later, but with nearly 40 years in this business I find I can't.

"To me it's time wasted when you sleep past six.

"In terms of hours on the job, at Kentucky and Texas A&M and those first few years at Alabama, I would say it took every hour other than about three in a twenty-four-hour day. The other three I just wasted. Taking a little nap," Bryant wrote several years ago.

Yet, hard work was not the only key to Bryant's success.

Talk to those whose lives he has touched and a common thread is woven through their comments: Paul Bryant makes people believe in themselves. He makes them believe they can succeed even when they lack the physical or mental abilities to do so.

Bryant has had his critics through the years. Some said he was brutal. Early in his career he was once accused of playing dirty football. It was even suggested that Alabama would be on probation within three years of Bryant's return, but that didn't happen.

But the harsh criticism has faded with time and accomplishments.

. . . Many good things have come my way, and I don't mind saying it's nice for people to think well of you, and it's nicer if a lot of people think a lot of you. I even get a kick out of those corny Bear Bryant jokes that make the rounds.

The worst one — and my preacher friends will have to pardon me — is about the guy who goes to Heaven and sees this very impressive figure with a white beard walking around a football field that has platinum stripes. The figure is wearing a cap with an A in red rubies on the peak.

The guy says, 'Who's that?'

And Saint Peter says, 'It's God, but He thinks He's Bear Bryant.'

— Bear

Tom Bailey

Some of Bear's Boys, including Coach Ray Perkins and members of Bryant's '82 team, paid their last respects.

Bear's Boys agree:
Nobody has ever done it better

"People asked me often about what it was like working for him. First of all, I never worked for him. I worked *with* him. The most special thing about the Bear was the way he treated people. He got people to do things. And he did that with a gentleness you'd never think the man had. Bear was one of those guys who'd stop by and say something special to his secretary, or to a player on the field. He always made you feel like you were the best player in the world."

— *Bum Phillips, former Texas A&M assistant and coach of the Houston Oilers, and now coach of the New Orleans Saints.*

• • •

"I've worked for Coach Bryant, and I've also worked for Barry Switzer, Johnny Majors and Chuck Fairbanks, some pretty good folks, and what distinguished him from the rest is that he was always on top of everything. I think the one area where he stood head and shoulders above the rest, was that he really, sincerely, cared about his players when they were there and after they were gone.

"My dad died when I was in the ninth grade and he was a friend of Coach Bryant's. Coach took me and paid my way through graduate school and then let me coach the freshman team. I quit football four years ago (under Oklahoma's Switzer) because I was awfully frustrated. Somehow he found me at a friend's house in Dallas, Texas, and told me I better get my rear back in coaching. He wanted me to come and stay with him.

"Now I'm back in it, and it's because of his genuine care for people."

— *Larry Lacewell, former Alabama assistant, and now coach at Arkansas State.*

• • •

"How did he do it? I've asked myself that. With the exception of one year at Texas A&M, we won everywhere while I was a player for him and later as a coach. I found out early under him what hard work was. He was one of the hardest working people in the profession. Once he got his program under way at Alabama, there was no way anybody was going to beat him at recruiting. And

Coach Bryant is welcomed to Dallas by Cotton Bowl
Vice President Jim Brock, 1980.

bat when we would meet every day and we better be there on time. Some coaches can tell you that, and it might not make an impression. It scared us to death. I would be a sophomore the next year and I wanted to play. I asked him what my chances were, because if I couldn't play much I was going to transfer. Coach Bryant told me that that was up to me, but the people who worked the hardest would be the people who played. I can still remember his exact words: 'Pardee, you work your butt off, then you'll damn sure play.'"

— *Jack Pardee, former Texas A&M player and later assistant and head pro coach.*

• • •

"Everytime some of us old players or some coaches who were under him get together, the talk has got to turn to Coach Bryant. There are always similar things in which he influenced us, yet it's surprising at the number of different ways he has touched the lives of people who played for him or coached under him. It was the little things he did, too, like taking time out of his schedule to congratulate our team for getting into the (NCAA Division II) playoffs. He was playing Auburn, the biggest week of the year for Alabama, and he called and chatted with me a few minutes."

— *Jim Fuller, former Alabama player and now coach at Jacksonville State.*

• • •

"Playing for Coach Bryant at Alabama was the thrill of my life, and the most memorable years of my life. The biggest and most lasting impression he made on me is the value of discipline. I'll never forget it, in life or in coaching."

— *Ray Perkins, former Alabama player and coach of the New York Giants, now coach at Alabama.*

• • •

"Everybody knows what an impact Coach Bryant has had on college football. He's done so much for the sport. But let me tell you, it's outside of football where recognition should go, too. It's where he helped a player or assistant coach the most. He helped you prepare for life. If you needed help, he was there. He was like your best friend."

— *Danny Ford, former Alabama player and now coach at Clemson.*

• • •

"It's been an honor for me to have been associated with Coach Bryant, as a player and then working with him on his staff. He has had a tremendous influence on my life, and certainly my coaching career. His compassion for his players is something I've tried to follow,

when nobody beats you, you're going to get good players. And when you get good players, you're going to win."

— *Jerry Claiborne, former Texas A&M player and assistant at Kentucky and Alabama, and now coach at Maryland.*

• • •

"When I went to West End High School in Birmingham, we didn't win many games; I think six in four years. When I went to Alabama, we lost two games in the three varsity years I was there. That's where I got exposed to an awful lot of success. When I left Alabama, I had the opportunity to work under Bud Wilkinson at Oklahoma, Paul Dietzel at West Point, and then Doug Dickey at Tennessee. I got to see three other guys at the top of their profession at that phase of their life. I got a chance to compare them with Coach Bryant. I learned something from all three, but Coach Bryant, by far and away, had the biggest impact on my coaching career and my life."

— *Bill Battle, former Alabama player and coach at Tennessee, and now a Selma businessman.*

• • •

"I grew up in Tuscaloosa, and that's

where I wanted to play my college ball. After graduation, Coach Bryant told me I wasn't good enough to play for him, because they were going with the drop-back passers like Namath and Stabler. I wasn't a drop-back passer, but you know what? Coach told me he'd help me somewhere else, and that's basically why I went to Virginia Tech. It's that kind of honesty that you appreciate. Then later, as an assistant at Alabama, I learned two things about coaching: One, I learned you change with the game. If your players are right for the wishbone, stay with the wishbone. If they're not, go to another offense. The second thing I learned under Coach Bryant was to always be prepared for everything. Nothing ever caught him by surprise."

— *Al Kincaid, former Alabama assistant and now coach at Wyoming.*

• • •

"I was a freshman at Texas A&M when we heard we were getting a new head coach. It was Coach Bryant. For some reason, there was about a two-month delay before he came, and a lot of students had to go ahead and make their class schedules. Some didn't. When he arrived, he told us right off the

Bryant at a Joe Namath "roast" with Dean Martin and Joe, 1974.

but no one can be a Coach Bryant."

— *Steve Sloan, former Alabama player and assistant, head coach at Vanderbilt, and now coach at Duke.*

• • •

"I believe that a big chunk of his success was that his players, as well as his coaches, didn't want to disappoint him. This is what leadership is all about. I know when I was a player, I didn't want to disappoint him. As a coach, I definitely didn't want to disappoint him with a performance. Coach Landry is very much like that.

"I know I picked up a great deal of things during my association with Coach Bryant. Intangibles. I know he influenced me as a coach by teaching me to never give up on your talent. And he told me there was no substitution for work. He

convinced his people. And when players and coaches are convinced they can win, they're going to win."

— *Gene Stallings, former Texas A&M player and head coach, and now defensive coach for the Dallas Cowboys.*

• • •

"When I think about what things made Coach Bryant a great coach, I think about the time I was a player at Alabama, and we just happened to be fortunate to play at a time when little guys could play. We won because he convinced all of us we were good players. I think that's the greatest quality he had. It wasn't until I got into coaching that I found out I wasn't a good football player. I don't think any coach in America would have given Charley Pell the chance he gave me."

— *Charley Pell, former Alabama player and coach at Clemson, and now coach at Florida.*

Bryant and new Alabama coach, Ray Perkins, 1982.

"*I don't want my players to be like any other students. I want special people.*"

Gene Stallings, Texas A&M coach, with his former boss, Paul Bryant, 1967.

Bryant's victory ride after beating Auburn for national title, 1964.
(#36 is Jackie Sherrill, #42 is Harold Moore; #78 is Lewis Thompson.)

The 300th win, 1980.

Bryant: The legend

Bryant with Richard Todd at the Sugar Bowl, 1976.

NEW TREASURED BILL

Bryant with the Kentucky Wildcats' mascot, who is eyeing Bear's 300-game card, 1980.

Winningest coach ever, Bryant, gives Tide reins to Ray Perkins

With no tears, and no one cheering, Paul W. Bryant announced on Dec. 15, 1982, his 25 years as head University of Alabama football coach was one game from the end.

A few minutes later the university's president Dr. Joab L. Thomas announced Walter Ray Perkins, former All-America end, head coach, New York Giants, as Bryant's field successor.

Bryant's final combat command would be when Alabama meets Illinois in the Memphis Liberty Bowl.

Wearing a red blazer, trying to look relaxed, Bryant read from a typewritten sheet he jestingly said had been composed by (wife) Mary Harmon.

"There comes a time," he read, "in every profession when you need to hang it up and that has come for me as head football coach at the University of Alabama.

"My main purpose as director of athletics and head football coach here has been to field the best possible team, to improve each player as a person and to produce citizens who will be a credit to our modern day society.

"We have been successful in most of those areas, but now I feel the time is right for a change in our football leadership.

"We lost two big football games this year that we should have won. And we played only four or five games like Bryant coached teams should play.

"I've done a poor job of coaching.

"This is my school, my alma mater, and I love it. And I love the players but in my opinion they deserve better coaching than they've been getting from me this year and my stepping down is an effort to see that they get better coaching from someone else.

"It has been a great joy for me personally, to have had the opportunity to coach at my alma mater. I know I will miss coaching but the thing I will miss most is the association I had with the players, the coaches, the competition, all those things that have made such a strong tradition at Alabama.

"I can't say enough about, or thank enough, the coaches who are with me now, and those who have been with me in the past.

"I plan to continue as director of athletics and pledge my support to my successor in every respect, and I want to emphasize this, particularly in recruiting.

"I also am thankful to have had the support of every president I've worked under at the University, including our current president, Dr. Joab L. Thomas."

In the question period the coach who went past Alonzo Stagg's 315-victory

Alabama vs. Houston, 1971.

Liberty Bowl, 1982.

Alabama defeated Arkansas in the 1980 Sugar Bowl.

Bryant with assistant coaches Sylvester Croom and Steve Hale, 1982.

mark last year, to a current 322, said that he had been considering retirement "every time I get way away from home."

The old coach termed the new one "a fine Christian gentleman. He was a little more mature when he was here than most players. . .

"He was a halfback as a freshman. Then he caught a pass in the spring and went head on with (defensive back) Billy Piper.

"We kept him out of football for a year, then put him at end. He had real stiff hands, like I had.

"But he became a great receiver because he worked so hard at it. He was a great team man, unselfish."

Someone asked if Bryant had accomplished all his goals. He mentioned a failure: "I didn't coach until I was 90."

It was mentioned that Bryant looked tired.

"I'm a tired old man," he smiled wanly, "but not tired of football."

Alf Van Hoose

"I'm sick and tired of hearing Paul Bryant, Paul Bryant. I'm tired of hearing 315. I've lost a lot more games than I've won. Players win games."

Bryant's final game as coach — the 1982 Liberty Bowl vs. Illinois.

Smile of the man who just took Stagg's record.

An era is over, but it'll never be forgotten

The show is over.

It was a heckuva theater, every minute, every gesture.

There was the entrance, the measured step of kingly command, the star arrived on stage.

There was the stately march around the playground, a one-man parade really.

And then the goal-post scene, his bit players eager and active, conscious of that penetrating gaze.

There was his sideline ritual, with rolled battleplan, the maestro conducting orchestration.

There were victories. Many, many. There were defeats. A few.

There was the exit, the face carved from Mount Rushmore registering lordly disdain of whatever the scoreboard showed, chin up, eyes front.

There was his palace guard, escorting royalty through the gathering mob.

Paul William Bryant, Arkansas son of the soil, Alabama's for a grand quarter-century, 1958-1982, is leaving the ring.

He departs as a champion. One year doesn't count. A lifetime does.

The legend doesn't end. It's for history.

Bryant on game day, combat site, was style. Style, alone, won't win. Many losers have style.

Substance will win. Bryant built substance first, discipline and order in himself, then into the boys he'd molded into the men he took to battle.

Always he spoke of class. His players performed with class, if they played.

"Be brave," Bill Battle tells it, "was always the last thing Coach would say as we left the dressing room before a game."

Alabama players played bravely, as did Texas A&M players and Kentucky players and Maryland players before them.

Bryant influenced every mama's and papa's son he coached, the vast majority of those thousands positively.

No prouder fraternity exists—though it's not formal — than those men, now scattered world-wide, composing the "I played for Coach Bryant" society.

Joe Namath is in it; Babe Parilli and John David Crow; Billy Neighbors and Snake Stabler; John Musso and Richard Todd.

Tom Boler and Woody Buchanan are in there, too, and Jim Duke and Danny Gilbert and Sam Maddox and hundreds of other Tiders without lasting field fame. They are also "my chillun" to The Man.

They also served. Bryant remembered.

And more and more, as the years rolled on, and wisdom increased, Bryant, though forever macho, spoke more and more of love to his players.

Sentiment and concern increasingly shared quarters with the competitive fire to excel that flamed inside the poor farmboy Hank Crisp drove into a new world, far from Fordyce, in 1931.

Bryant did care — else why would he demand 100 percent from players? Anything less, he knew, would be cheating.

So, an era ends. There is sadness.

There would be tears. From Bryant, too. He was not ashamed to cry.

He had to be hoping he made a sound decision. It would be second-guessed.

A generation has turned, another launched since he returned to Tuscaloosa nearly 25 years ago. Thousands know no Alabama football except Bear Bryant Alabama football.

Say this for those: They knew the best.

They knew a coach, but more than that, they knew a man.

Alf Van Hoose

Howard Cosell awaited an interview with Paul Bryant.

Reggie Jackson and Paul Bryant visited during a Yankee exhibition game in Tuscaloosa, 1978.

Bryant with golfer Kathy Whitworth, 1972.

Coaches Bear Bryant and Dan Devine, 1981.

Bryant with Nebraska's Bob Devaney at Miami, 1971.

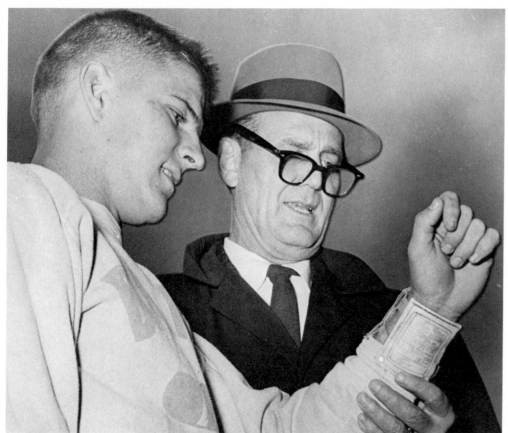

Coach Bryant with Pat Trammell at the Liberty Bowl
in Philadelphia, 1959.

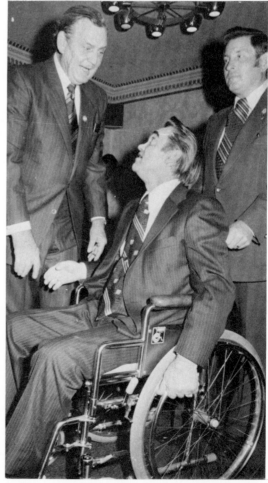

Gov. George Wallace was guest speaker at
a dinner in Bryant's honor, 1975.

Bryant with Auburn quarterback Pat Sullivan
at premiere of Namath film, 1971.

*"It's a fine day. Interest rates are
down, the weather is beautiful, the
World Series is about to come on and
we get to play Ole Miss at home."*

Bryant on sideline with offensive coordinator Mal Moore.

Heart attack ends life of legendary Bear Bryant

Paul William "Bear" Bryant, who carried the University of Alabama to the heights of football greatness, died Wednesday, Jan. 26, 1983, in a Tuscaloosa hospital.

The 69-year-old Bryant, who retired in December after 25 years as the Crimson Tide's head coach, reportedly suffered a massive heart attack shortly after noon while receiving an X-ray at Druid City Hospital.

At 12:24 p.m., Bryant had a sudden cardio-pulmonary arrest. Resuscitation measures were carried out—including the insertion of a pacemaker into his chest — but all measures were unsuccessful. Bryant was pronounced dead at 1:30 p.m.

Cause of death was listed as a massive coronary occlusion—a blockage that interferes with coronary arteries supplying the heart with blood.

Bryant had checked into the hospital Tuesday night with chest pains. Bryant's physician, Dr. William Hill, told *The Birmingham News* that night that Bryant had been placed in the coronary care unit and that he was under observation "as a precautionary measure."

A hospital spokesman said Bryant spent a restful Tuesday night, and Hill said Bryant's vital signs were stable and that his electrocardiogram appeared normal.

In Montgomery, Lt. Gov. Bill Baxley, an Alabama alumnus and graduate of its law school, broke the news to the Senate at 2:10 p.m.

A moment later, Sen. Ryan DeGraffenried from Tuscaloosa rose and asked that the flag atop the state capital be lowered to half staff "in recognition of this great man."

"He probably contributed more to the University of Alabama and the education of young men in this state than anyone I've ever known."

Sugar Bowl, 1979.

"It doesn't matter whether I continue to work or have to retire and work for free. I can do either one. Of course, the good Lord will have the final say on the matter."

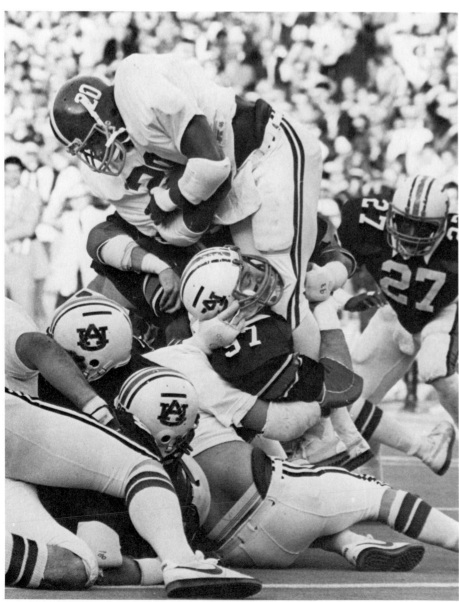

Ken Simon (20) is on top during the 1981 Alabama-Auburn game.

Bryant received congratulations from President Ronald Reagan for breaking Amos Alonzo Stagg's record, 1981.

"Don't lose your game at the half. Concentrate on winning in the second half. Don't waste time on stuff that can't help you."

Bryant walked to the dressing room following the Cotton Bowl game, 1982.

Bryant announced his retirement, 1982.

BEAR MOUNTAIN

A final message to Coach Bryant was hung from an interstate overpass.

The final audience for Bryant

"Paul," begins a white-bearded Duff Daugherty quip, oft-quoted, "you might not be the best coach in the country but you sure attract attention."

Paul W. Bryant, a few years later was, indisputably, America's No. 1 college coach. He continued attracting attention, and crowds.

Alabama's legendary man attracted final audiences, too. They mustered for a last salute in Tuscaloosa and Birmingham.

Daugherty, then at Michigan State, now retired to California, was scheduled to be among them. Early week plans had Bear and Duff pairing for Super Bowl commentary in Las Vegas' Riviera Hotel.

President Ronald Reagan wasn't at Bryant services. He offered to be here, however, to Mrs. Bryant over a Wednesday phone.

"Mama told him we appreciated that," Mae Martin Bryant Tyson said

Thursday, "but he ought to stay in Washington."

Billy Graham, world evangelist, had offered, over another phone, to fly in and conduct the funeral services.

"It would have meant Mr. Graham canceling three Crusade services," Mrs. Tyson told it. "Goodness knows, Mama didn't want him to do that."

But paths, air and ground, to somber-skied Tuscaloosa Thursday had their traffic.

John McKay came up from Tampa; Bum Phillips from New Orleans. Charley Pell flew up from Gainesville, Fla; Steve Sloan from Durham, N.C.

A private plane from Dallas had another coach, Gene Stallings, as well as a former player, Lee Roy Jordan, and an

A moment of sadness at the cemetery.

Lee Roy Jordan, ex-linebacker with the Dallas Cowboys; Charlie Pell, head coach at the University of Florida, and John David Crow, Bryant's only Heisman winner, at Bryant's funeral.

All-America Bama alumnus Dave Cowden.

There were Bryant stories told on that airship, one of them by Jordan, who became a Bryant textbook model for courage and class.

"I called Coach not long after the Auburn game," Jordan said. "He told me about a strange dream.

"He said he had dreamed he retired and died a week later."

Bryant Kentucky alumni Jim Proffitt and Joe Koch had not talked with their coach in months. But they came Thursday.

"We're here," Louisville merchant prince Proffitt declared, "because of love for Coach Bryant, respect for his family, and because we want anyone from Alabama, Maryland or Texas A&M to know Kentuckians loved him just as strongly as they did.

"There'll be a bunch of us down. Al Zampino, Allen Hamilton and John Miehaus are already here."

Koch is a manufacturer of air filters with sales to 14 countries.

"I knew I was a man after playing for Coach Bryant," Koch said. "Business was easy after he finished with me.

"And let me tell you this. I was captain of our (1954) team under Blanton Collier, after Coach Bryant left for Texas A&M.

"Every Friday, before a game, I'd get a telegram from Coach Bryant wishing the team success. I'd read it to the team in the dressing room."

Jordan has a host of company from Alabama's Bryant men: Billy Neighbors, Fred Sington Jr., Phil Dabbs, Jerry Duncan, Steve Bowman, Scott Hunter and Benny Nelson in a visiting vanguard.

There were also stories, most starring the man in his various roles as dictator or servant, or five-star general or corporal; judge and jury, or confesser of wrongdoing.

The world knew him best as Bear Bryant. To his family of men, proudest of societies, it's only 'Coach Bryant.'

Not once during a long, long day did I hear a former player of Bryant use the word 'Bear'.

Only 'Coach Bryant'.

Doesn't that tell a story, too?

Alf Van Hoose

Former Alabama quarterback Steadman Shealy delivered a
eulogy at a memorial service on the school's campus
for Coach Bryant.

*This young man paid his
last respects to the Bear at the cemetery.*

Students at Alabama shortly after they learned of Bryant's death.

Solemn, silent, sad: Campus says goodbye to Bryant

He was a burly young man with thick neck and broad shoulders, and at another time and place the tears in his eyes might have looked a little odd.

But not Thursday in Memorial Coliseum, where he was just one of some 6,000 University of Alabama faculty members, students and townspeople who gathered to pay homage to Paul W. Bryant.

The memorial service was held mainly for University students and personnel, as Bryant's body lay in state at nearby Hayes Chapel in Tuscaloosa awaiting his funeral, followed by his burial in Elmwood Cemetery in Birmingham.

The crowd — mostly young people, solemn-faced and sad — started trickling into the 15,000-seat Coliseum well before the service began, and then came in streams.

There was little talk, even as they took their seats.

The faces of the young men and women seemed to say, "Talk is cheap. We came here to mourn for our coach."

About the only sounds in the Coliseum were the prayers and remarks made by those involved in the ceremony.

A telegram to Mrs. Mary Harmon Bryant from evangelist Billy Graham, in which Graham said he and the famous coach had been "friends for years," was read aloud to the silent gathering.

In the telegram to the widow, Graham said Bryant himself "felt unworthy spiritually," but then added that the winningest college coach in history had a "deep faith in God."

Steadman Shealy, former quarterback and constant companion of Bryant in recent years, also centered his

Alabama football players carried Bryant's casket from the church.

Crowds filled the cemetery on the day of Bryant's burial.

remarks on Bryant's faith in God.

In the dressing room at the Liberty Bowl game, Shealy said Bryant got down on his knees and thanked God for his years of association with football and the University of Alabama.

"The greatest coach who ever lived was not too proud to get on his knees," said Shealy. "He prayed, 'Lord, thank you for allowing me to be with football, to be with this team and with this University these many years.'"

Shealy said he felt that this former coach was in heaven and praised him for the many things he did for all his football players and those who worked under him.

"He gave us something very few people can give — he gave us himself," said Shealy, who added that he and Bryant often talked about "God, prayer and Jesus Christ."

Shealy said Bryant once said to him, "Steadman, you know that I probably pray more than you do. I never see a handicapped person that I don't pray for them."

Bryant recently told him, said Shealy, that he wanted to "become a better Christian."

Shealy said he was convinced that his former coach is now a winner with God, just as he was a winner here on earth.

Perhaps Bryant's greatest quality, he added, was that he taught his players to be a whole person, "physically, mentally and spiritually."

"He taught me a lot — how to be a champion. He prepared me not only to be a football player but after football, too," he said.

The ceremony ended with the singing of the alma mater.

Few members of the crowd joined in, even though invited to do so by Edwin Weaver, a music student at the University.

Some said later that they were too shocked to sing.

The crowd stood and waited, in further silence, as the Bryant family left; then the remaining mourners filed out, the only sound coming from the shuffling of thousands of feet.

Harold Kennedy

HIS PERMANENT HAT RACK

COLLEGE FOOTBALL

BROOK THE BIRMINGHAM NEWS

Remembering the man.

He could have coached 38 more, and it wouldn't have been too much

NEW YORK — He smoked too much. If the pocket was Bear Bryant's you could bet it held a crumpled pack of cigarettes.

He drank too much. When he came to New York a couple of years ago to address The Associated Press Board of Directors, his attache case contained a bottle of vodka.

He partied too much. A few Aprils back, when he was hospitalized during spring practice, I asked him what the doctors had diagnosed.

"They said it was 75 percent smoking, 20 percent diet and 5 percent booze and other stuff," he replied.

"I wish," he added almost wistfully, "I wish it had been 75 percent of that booze and other stuff."

Bear Bryant wasn't a saint. He was a head football coach, for 38 years. He could have coached 38 more, and it wouldn't have been too much. "Too much ain't ever enough," one of Bryant's "pupils" once said.

A letter should have arrived in Bryant's office by now. I mailed it Monday, the day before he entered the hospital. It told the Bear what I somehow neglected to tell him during our last visit, an hour-long private get-together in his Memphis hotel suite the day before the Liberty Bowl, his 323rd and last victory.

It said what a privilege it had been to cover Alabama and Bryant so often, especially during the countdown to his breaking Amos Alonzo Stagg's record of

314 coaching victories.

I wrote that I intended to take him up on his blanket offer to the media to "break bread" with him in Tuscaloosa. Hopefully, I said, we might even try and break par if the torn ligaments in his left arm allowed him to swing a golf club.

The letter will go unanswered now, but I have a feeling Coach Bryant — I could never bring myself to address him as anything other than "Coach" — will read it, and read between the lines how much he meant to so many of us.

Oh yes, the Bear knew what the media needed and how to provide it, especially when it served his purpose.

"Sit down, boy," he snapped — I was 47 at the time — the day I started to explain that I had planned to be in

Bryant congratulated Reggie Collier after Southern Mississippi beat Alabama, 1982.

"I have tried to teach them to show class, to have pride and to display character. I think football, winning games, takes care of itself if you do that."

Tuscaloosa that particular week, long before a story broke in Atlanta charging racial dissension on the Alabama team.

"I'm through tip-toeing around and I'm through pussy-footing around," he growled. "I'm going back to being Paul Bryant and anybody who doesn't like the way Paul Bryant does things can get out of here."

He went on like that for a while. Then he paused, smiled sheepishly, and said, "I don't really know what I'm trying to say."

Of course, he knew full well what he was doing, giving me a national headline-making story. It even made *The Tuscaloosa News,* Alabama's hometown newspaper.

Later, Al Browning, the paper's sports editor, told me, "He told me the same things earlier in the week and said if I wrote it, he'd kill me."

I remember him towering over most people at 6-foot-4, but never looking down on anyone.

I remember him and John Wayne, sitting on the same couch, both slightly

smashed.

I remember he almost ran me over with a golf cart at practice one day, then told me — ordered me — to hop in and asked, "Do any of those other (blankety-blank) coaches give you this kind of service?"

I remember him putting his arm around Johnny Majors a few days before the 1976 Pitt-Georgia Sugar Bowl, Majors' last game as Pitt coach before going to Tennessee and drawling, "Welcome to the SEC son."

I remember how he never let me forget that in 1966, Alabama was No. 1 in the pre-season AP poll, went 11-0, and finished third. It cost him an unprecedented third straight national championship.

I remember his shuffling along the sidelines, the lined face under the houndstooth hat, the rolled-up program in his hand, scheming up ways to win still another game. And I remember that stretch when the Bear forgot how to "win the big one" and I covered a half-dozen or more games without seeing

On the Sugar Bowl sidelines, 1980.

Alabama win. "Shoot," he would snort, "are you here again?"

Those things are all gone now and the Bear's work is done. Ironic how many times his friends used to sit around and wonder if he would ever retire. The consensus was that he would die within a year if he stopped coaching.

It didn't take that long. There was no spring practice to plan and someone else is on the recruiting trail for Alabama and it was all strange to the Bear. "This (victory) will make my future years — or

year — more pleasant," he said prophetically after the Liberty Bowl.

As they said on the farms of Bryant's Arkansas boyhood when the planting was done, the crop has been "laid by." And Bear Bryant, who always said he had a plan for everything — a plan for winning and a plan for losing — was left without a plan for coaching. And that left him without any plan at all.

Herschel Nissenson
AP sports writer

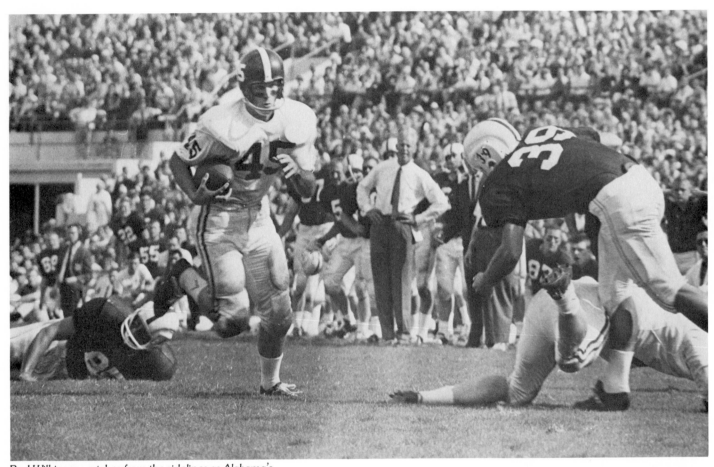

Bud Wilkinson watches from the sidelines as Alabama's Cotton Clark (45) runs for a TD against Oklahoma in the 1963 Orange Bowl.

"Don't do a lot of coaching just before the game. If you haven't coached them by 14 minutes to two on Saturday, it's too late then."

Alabama's Ken Stabler (12) in the 1968 Cotton Bowl vs. Texas A&M.

"I used to be one of the best (coaches), but now I'm not even a good coach anymore. But I know what it takes to win. I've made so many mistakes that if I don't make the same mistakes over, we're going to come pretty close to winning."

Coach Bryant and Coach Sloan, 1981.

Auburn's Barfield, Alabama's Bryant, 1979.

Bryant with Baylor's Geff Gandy, 1979.

The Alabama coaching staff offered encouragement from the sidelines.

Coach Bryant with quarterback Walter Lewis.

Reflections on a hero

The body of Paul Bryant rests in Elmwood and his spirit is caught up in the great promise.

Now it's possible to reflect on both the man and the impact he had on all who knew him in the many ways there are to know a man.

The outpouring of love, affection, respect and grief for the Bear was a human phenomenon not often witnessed in this day of cynicism, avarice and anxiety.

The death of this good man cut through the crippling web of moral failure and loose discipline that has beset the country during the past 20 years to touch people as they have not been touched in decades.

How is it, you may ask, that the coach of a sometimes despised macho sport commanded so much love and loyalty? Was it real or was it sheer gossamer? Was the outpouring for a real human being or for a straw figure created by a slavish devotion to sport and effective imagemakers?

He was real. Not perfect, but real. And it was this quality that opened him to people and people to him. There was a kind of coherence and wholeness to his life that people from all walks of life recognized instinctively. There was also grace, a grace that was a rare mixture of humility and pride which allowed him to accept both victory and defeat philosophically.

He was one of the most successful coaches of all time, but he did not abandon the principles that were central to his understanding of life to obtain success.

He raised coaching men to the level of art. In so doing, he demonstrated to young and old that the principles which win football games are the same ones that win worthwhile goals and struggles in the larger world.

He was a hero. He did not slay dragons, but he conquered the biggest opponent he probably ever met — himself — and was freed thereafter to become the real human being he was.

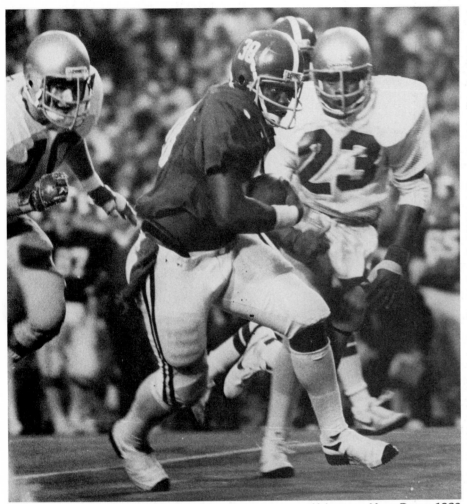

Alabama vs. Notre Dame, 1980.

One can say all this, and still the mystery remains: How one man could touch the hearts and imaginations of so many.

But of one aspect, we are sure! The outpouring of love and grief for the Bear has to say something good about the thousands of Alabamians who feel his loss. All those who mourn his death have something of his quality, too, else they may not have recognized it in him.

Editorial

Directing traffic during 315th win.

Coach Bryant with Robbie Jones, 1981.

After the Alabama-Tennessee game, 1974.

Bryant displayed his skill at dominoes, 1979.

Bryant with Jets' Lou Holtz, 1976.

Bryant with LSU coach Jerry Stovall, 1982.

Bryant with some of the Junction Boys at 1979 reunion.

"I had no doubt we would win at Alabama. I just didn't know how long it would take."

Bryant got a happy, bumpy ride from his Bama charges, 1978.

Action in the 1981 Alabama-Auburn game —
Bryant's 315th win.

"Don't give up before the game starts. I lost a Kentucky game with Georgia in 1946 simply because I didn't believe we could win."

The 315th win, 1981.

Ricky Moore (26) with the ball (Alabama vs. Auburn, 1981).

Bear always had a poem with him

Tram Sessions, a former legislator from Birmingham, clipped a poem from a magazine and mailed it to Coach Paul "Bear" Bryant.

Bryant became fond of the poem, written by W. Heartsill Wilson, and always carried it in his wallet, Sessions said.

This is the poem:

This is the beginning of a new day.

God has given me this day to use as I will.

I can waste it or use it for good.

What I do today is very important because I am

Exchanging a day of my life for it.

When tomorrow comes, this day will be gone forever.

Leaving something in its place I have traded for it.

I want it to be a gain, not loss — good, not evil.

Success, not failure in order that I

Shall not forget the price I paid for it.

Bryant on sideline during 1970
defeat to Southern Cal.

*Major Ogilvie (42) on a TD run in the
Alabama-Southern Cal game, 1978.*

Steadman Shealy (10) with the ball in the 1980 Sugar Bowl.

The funeral procession passed Bryant-Denny Stadium in Tuscaloosa.

*Coach Bryant lost his chef's hat as he and Ara Parseghian of Notre Dame
stirred cafe brulot before the Sugar Bowl in New Orleans, 1973.*

Bear Stats

Bryant's year-by-year record
Won 323, Lost 85, Tied 17

At MARYLAND
1945 (6-2-1)

60	Guilford	6
21	Richmond	0
22	Merchant Marine	6
13	Virginia Poly	21
13	West Virginia	13
14	Wm & Mary	33
38	VMI	0
19	Virginia	13
19	South Carolina	13

At KENTUCKY
(8 years, 60-23-5)
1946 (7-3)

20	Mississippi	6
26	Cincinnati	7
70	Xavier	0
13	Georgia	28
10	Vanderbilt	7
7	Alabama	21
39	Michigan State	14
35	Marquette	7
13	West Virginia	0
0	Tennessee	7

1947 (8-3)

7	Mississippi	14
20	Cincinnati	0
20	Xavier	7
26	Georgia	0
14	Vanderbilt	0
7	Michigan State	6
0	Alabama	13
15	West Virginia	6
36	Evansville	0
6	Tennessee	13

Great Lakes Bowl

24	Virginia	14

1948 (5-3-2)

48	Xavier	7
7	Mississippi	20
12	Georgia	35
7	Vanderbilt	26
25	Marquette	0
28	Cincinnati	7
13	Villanova	13
34	Florida	15
0	Tennessee	0
25	Miami	5

1949 (9-3)

71	So. Mississippi	7
19	LSU	0
47	Mississippi	0
25	Georgia	0
44	The Citadel	0
7	SMU	20
14	Cincinnati	7
21	Xavier	7
35	Florida	0
0	Tennessee	6
21	Miami	6

Orange Bowl

13	Santa Clara	21

1950 (11-1)

Paul Bryant and Adolph Rupp at a dinner in their honor at Lexington, Ky., 1946.

(SEC Champions)

25	No. Texas St.	0
14	LSU	0
27	Mississippi	0
40	Dayton	0
41	Cincinnati	7
34	Villanova	7
28	Georgia Tech	14
40	Florida	6
48	Mississippi State	21
83	North Dakota	0
0	Tennessee	7

Sugar Bowl

13	Oklahoma	7

1951 (8-4)

72	Tennessee Tech	13
6	Texas	7
17	Mississippi	21
7	Georgia Tech	13
27	Mississippi State	0
35	Villanova	13
14	Florida	6
32	Miami	0
37	Tulane	0
47	George Washington	13
0	Tennessee	28

Cotton Bowl

20	TCU	7

1952 (5-4-2)

6	Villanova	25
13	Mississippi	13
10	Texas A&M	7
7	LSU	34
14	Mississippi State	27
14	Cincinnati	6
29	Miami	0
27	Tulane	6
27	Clemson	14
14	Tennessee	14
0	Florida	27

1953 (7-2-1)

6	Texas A&M	7

6	Mississippi	22
26	Florida	13
6	LSU	6
32	Mississippi State	13
19	Villanova	0
19	Rice	13
40	Vanderbilt	17
20	Memphis State	7
27	Tennessee	21

At TEXAS A&M
(4 years, 25-14-2)
1954 (1-9)

9	Texas Tech	41
6	Oklahoma State	14
6	Georgia	0
7	Houston	10
20	TCU	21
7	Baylor	20
7	Arkansas	14
3	SMU	6
19	Rice	29
13	Texas	22

1955 (7-2-1)

0	UCLA	21
28	LSU	0
21	Houston	3
27	Nebraska	0
19	TCU	16
19	Baylor	7
7	Arkansas	7
13	SMU	2
20	Rice	12
6	Texas	21

1956 (9-0-1)
(SWC Champions)

19	Villanova	0
9	LSU	6
40	Texas Tech	7
14	Houston	14
7	TCU	6
19	Baylor	13
27	Arkansas	0
33	SMU	7
21	Rice	7
34	Texas	21

1957 (8-3-0)

21	Maryland	13
21	Texas Tech	0
28	Missouri	6
28	Houston	6
7	TCU	0
14	Baylor	0
7	Arkansas	6
19	SMU	6
6	Rice	7
7	Texas	9

Gator Bowl

0	Tennessee	3

At ALABAMA
(25 years, 232-46-9)
1958 (5-4-1)

3	LSU	13
0	Vanderbilt	0
29	Furman	6
7	Tennessee	14
9	Mississippi State	7
12	Georgia	0
7	Tulane	13
17	Georgia Tech	8
14	Memphis State	0
8	Auburn	14

1959 (7-2-2)

3	Georgia	17
3	Houston	0
7	Vanderbilt	7
13	Chattanooga	0
7	Tennessee	7
10	Mississippi State	0
19	Tulane	7
9	Georgia Tech	7
14	Memphis State	7
10	Auburn	0

Liberty Bowl

0	Penn State	7

1960 (8-1-2)

21	Georgia	6
6	Tulane	6
21	Vanderbilt	0
7	Tennessee	20
14	Houston	0
7	Mississippi State	0
51	Furman	0
16	Georgia Tech	15
34	Tampa	6
3	Auburn	0

Bluebonnet Bowl

3	Texas	3

1961 (11-0-0)
(National Champions)
(SEC Champions)

32	Georgia	6
9	Tulane	0
35	Vanderbilt	6

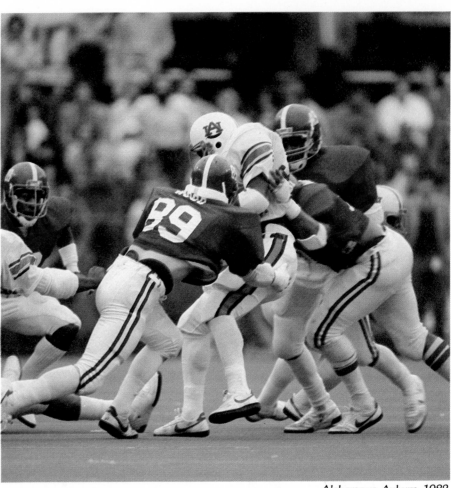

Alabama vs. Auburn, 1982.

26	N.C. State	7
34	Tennessee	3
17	Houston	0
24	Mississippi State	0
66	Richmond	0
10	Georgia Tech	0
34	Auburn	0

Sugar Bowl

10	Arkansas	3

1962 (10-1)

35	Georgia	0
44	Tulane	6
17	Vanderbilt	7
14	Houston	3
27	Tennessee	7
35	Tulsa	6
20	Mississippi State	0
36	Miami	3
6	Georgia Tech	7
38	Auburn	0

Orange Bowl

17	Oklahoma	0

1963 (9-2)

32	Georgia	7
28	Tulane	0
21	Vanderbilt	6
6	Florida	10
35	Tennessee	0
21	Houston	13
20	Mississippi State	19
27	Georgia Tech	11
8	Auburn	10

Paul Bryant and Darrell Royal had to share a trophy following the Bluebonnet Bowl in 1960.

17	Miami	12

Sugar Bowl

12	Mississippi	7

1964 (10-1)
(National Champions)
(SEC Champions

31	Georgia	3
36	Tulane	6
24	Vanderbilt	0
21	N.C. State	0
19	Tennessee	8
17	Florida	14
23	Mississippi State	6
17	LSU	9
24	Georgia Tech	7
21	Auburn	14

Orange Bowl

17	Texas	21

1965 (9-1-1)
(National Champions)
(SEC Champions)

17	Georgia	18
27	Tulane	0
17	Mississippi	16

22	Vanderbilt	7
7	Tennessee	7
21	Florida State	0
10	Mississippi State	7
31	LSU	7
35	South Carolina	14
30	Auburn	3

Orange Bowl

39	Nebraska	28

1966 (11-0)
(SEC Champions)

34	Louisiana Tech	0
17	Mississippi	7
26	Clemson	0
11	Tennessee	10
42	Vanderbilt	6
27	Mississippi State	14
21	LSU	0
24	South Carolina	0
34	So. Mississippi	0
31	Auburn	0

Sugar Bowl

34	Nebraska	7

1967 (8-2-1)

37	Florida State	37
25	So. Mississippi	3
21	Mississippi	7
35	Vanderbilt	21
13	Tennessee	24
13	Clemson	10
13	Mississippi State	0
7	LSU	6
17	South Carolina	0
7	Auburn	3

Cotton Bowl

16	Texas A&M	20

1968 (8-3)

14	Virginia Tech	7
17	So. Mississippi	14
8	Mississippi	10
31	Vanderbilt	7
9	Tennessee	10
21	Clemson	14
20	Mississippi State	13
16	LSU	7
14	Miami	6
24	Auburn	16

Gator Bowl

10	Missouri	35

1969 (6-5)

17	Virginia Tech	13
63	So. Mississippi	14
33	Mississippi	32
10	Vanderbilt	14
14	Tennessee	41
38	Clemson	13
23	Mississippi State	19
15	LSU	20
42	Miami	6
26	Auburn	49

Liberty Bowl

33	Colorado	47

1970 (6-5-1)

21	Southern Cal	42
51	Virginia Tech	18
46	Florida	15
23	Mississippi	48
35	Vanderbilt	11
0	Tennessee	24
30	Houston	21
35	Mississippi State	6
9	LSU	14
32	Miami	8
28	Auburn	33

Astro-Bluebonnet Bowl

24	Oklahoma	24

1971 (11-1)

17	Southern Cal	10
42	So. Mississippi	6
38	Florida	0
40	Mississippi	6
42	Vanderbilt	0
32	Tennessee	15
34	Houston	20
41	Mississippi State	10
14	LSU	7
31	Miami	3
31	Auburn	7

Orange Bowl

6	Nebraska	38

1972 (10-2)
(SEC Champions)

35	Duke	12
35	Kentucky	0

Coach Bryant with his new Tide staff in 1958. From left, Sam Bailey, Phil Cutchin, Jerry Claiborne, Elmer Smith, Pat James, Carney Laslie.

48	Vanderbilt	21
25	Georgia	7
24	Florida	7
17	Tennessee	10
48	So. Mississippi	11
58	Mississippi State	14
35	LSU	21
52	Virginia Tech	13
16	Auburn	17

Cotton Bowl

13	Texas	17

1973 (11-1)
(UPI National Champions)
(SEC Champions)

66	California	0
28	Kentucky	14
44	Vanderbilt	0
28	Georgia	14
35	Florida	14
42	Tennessee	21
77	Virginia Tech	6
35	Mississippi State	0
43	Miami	13
21	LSU	7
35	Auburn	0

Sugar Bowl

23	Notre Dame	24

1974 (11-1)
(SEC Champions)

21	Maryland	16
52	So. Mississippi	0

23	Vanderbilt	10
35	Mississippi State	21
8	Florida State	7
28	Tennessee	6
41	TCU	3
35	Mississippi State	0
30	LSU	0
28	Miami	7
17	Auburn	13

Orange Bowl

11	Notre Dame	13

1975 (11-1)
(SEC Champions)

7	Missouri	20
56	Clemson	0
40	Vanderbilt	7
32	Ole Miss	6
52	Washington	0
30	Tennessee	7
45	TCU	0
21	Mississippi State	10
23	LSU	10
27	So. Mississippi	6
28	Auburn	0

Sugar Bowl

13	Penn State	6

1976 (9-3)

7	Mississippi	10
56	SMU	3
42	Vanderbilt	14
0	Georgia	21

24	So. Mississippi	8
20	Tennessee	13
24	LSU	3
34	Mississippi State	17
28	LSU	17
18	Notre Dame	21
38	Auburn	7

Liberty Bowl

36	UCLA	6

1977 (11-1)
(SEC Champions)

34	Mississippi	13
24	Nebraska	31
24	Vanderbilt	12
18	Georgia	10
21	Southern Cal	20
24	Tennessee	10
55	Louisville	6
37	Mississippi State	7
24	LSU	3
36	Miami	0
48	Auburn	21

Sugar Bowl

35	Ohio State	6

1978 (11-1)
(AP National Champions)
(SEC Champions)

20	Nebraska	3
38	Missouri	20
14	Southern Cal	24
51	Vanderbilt	28

20	Washington	17
23	Florida	12
30	Tennessee	17
35	Virginia Tech	0
35	Mississippi State	14
31	LSU	10
34	Auburn	16

Sugar Bowl

14	Penn State	7

1979 (12-0)
(National Champions)
(SEC Champions)

30	Georgia Tech	6
45	Baylor	0
66	Vanderbilt	3
38	Wichita State	0
40	Florida	0
27	Tennessee	17
31	Virginia Tech	7
24	Mississippi State	7
3	LSU	0
30	Miami	0
25	Auburn	18

Sugar Bowl

24	Arkansas	9

1980 (10-2)

26	Georgia Tech	3
59	Mississippi	35
41	Vanderbilt	0
45	Kentucky	0
17	Rutgers	13
27	Tennessee	0
42	So. Mississippi	7
3	Mississippi State	6
28	LSU	7
0	Notre Dame	7
34	Auburn	18

Cotton Bowl

30	Baylor	2

1981 (9-2-1)
(SEC Champions)

24	LSU	7
21	Georgia Tech	24
19	Kentucky	10
28	Vanderbilt	7
38	Ole Miss	7
13	So. Mississippi	13
38	Tennessee	19
31	Rutgers	7
13	Mississippi State	10
31	Penn State	16
28	Auburn	17

Cotton Bowl

12	Texas	14

1982 (8-4)

45	Georgia Tech	7
42	Ole Miss	14
24	Vanderbilt	21
34	Arkansas State	7
42	Penn State	21
28	Tennessee	35
21	Cincinnati	7
20	Mississippi State	12
10	LSU	20
29	So. Mississippi	38
22	Auburn	23

Liberty Bowl

21	Illinois	15

COACH BRYANT'S MILESTONE VICTORIES

No.	1	Maryland, 60-6 over Guilford College in 1945
No.	100	Alabama, 19-7 over Tulane in 1959
No.	150	Alabama, 24-7 over Georgia Tech in 1964
No.	200	Alabama, 17-10 over Southern Cal in 1971
No.	250	Alabama, 23-10 over LSU in 1975
No.	275	Alabama, 38-20 over Missouri in 1978
No.	285	Alabama, 30-6 over Georgia Tech in 1979
No.	290	Alabama, 27-17 over Tennessee in 1979
No.	295	Alabama, 25-18 over Auburn in 1979
No.	300	Alabama, 45-0 over Kentucky in 1980
No.	305	Alabama, 34-18 over Auburn in 1980
No.	310	Alabama, 38-7 over Mississippi in 1981
No.	314	Alabama, 31-6 over Penn State in 1981
No.	315	Alabama, 28-17 over Auburn in 1981
No.	323	Alabama, 21-15 over Illinois in 1982

BEAR'S BOYS
Bryant associates who became head coaches
(Total 44, college or professional)

Name	Head Coach For	School	Player-Coach
Mickey Andrews	y-North Alabama	Alabama	Player
Bill Arnsparger	New York Giants	Kentucky	Player
Bill Battle	Tennessee	Alabama	Player
Jim Blevins	Jacksonville State	Alabama	Both
x-Clark Boler	Bloomsburg St.	Alabama	Player
C. Bradshaw	y-Troy State	Ky. A&M, Ala.	Both
Ray Callahan	Cincinnati	Kentucky	Player
x-Jerry Claiborne	Kentucky	Ky. & Alabama	Both
John David Crow	Northeast Louisiana	A&M, Ala.	Both
Phil Cutchin	Oklahoma State	Ky. A&M, Ala.	Both
Paul Dietzel	y-South Carolina	Kentucky	Coach
x-Pat Dye	y-Auburn	Alabama	Coach
Bill Elias	Virginia	Maryland	Coach
x-Danny Ford	Clemson	Alabama	Both
x-Jimmy Fuller	Jacksonville State	Alabama	Player
Bill Hannah	Fullerton (Cal.) JC	Alabama	Player
Tom Harper	Wake Forest	Kentucky	Player
Wilbur Jamerson	Morehead (Ky.) State	Kentucky	Player
x-Al Kincaid	Wyoming	Alabama	Coach
J.T. King	Texas Tech	Texas A&M	Coach
x-Larry Lacewell	Arkansas State	Alabama	Coach
Key Meyer	San Francisco 49ers	Alabama	Coach
C. McClendon	LSU	Kentucky	Both
Jim McKenzie	Oklahoma	Kentucky	Player
Bud Moore	Kansas	Alabama	Both
F. Moseley	Virginia Tech	Maryland & Ky.	Coach
x-Bill Oliver	UT-Chattanooga	Alabama	Both
Jim Owens	Washington	Texas A&M	Coach
Jack Pardee	y-Wash. Redskins	Texas A&M	Player
Vito (Babe) Parilli	y-Chicago Wind	Kentucky	Player
x-Charley Pell	y-Florida	Alabama	Player
x-Ray Perkins	Alabama	Alabama	Player
x-Bum Phillips	New Orleans Saints	Texas A&M	Coach
Don Robbins	Idaho	Texas A&M	Player
x-H. S'berger	Miami	Ky. & Alabama	Both
Jimmy Sharpe	Virginia Tech	Alabama	Both
x-Jackie Sherrill	y-Texas A&M	Alabama	Player
x-Steve Sloan	y-Duke	Alabama	Both
Gene Stallings	Texas A&M	A&M & Alabama	Both
x-Jim Stanley	y-Michigan Panthers	Texas A&M	Player
Loyd Taylor	Tarleton (Tex.) State	Texas A&M	Player
x-Bob Tyler	y-No. Texas State	Alabama	Coach
R. Williamson	Memphis State	Alabama	Both
Jim Wright	Wichita State	Texas A&M	Player

x-Active Head Coach   y-Head Coach more than one team, one listed is last.